Contents

Hauntings Resolved

A Step by Step Guide to Soul Rescue

Penny Barber

Eloquent Books
New York, New York

Eloquent Books
An imprint of AEG Publishing Group
845 Third Avenue, 6th Floor - 6016
New York, NY 10022
www.eloquentbooks.com

ISBN: 978-1-60860-565-1

Printed in the United States of America

Book Design: Rolando F. Santos

PENNY BARBER is a time served Spiritualist Medium, working as an Accredited Demonstrator for the S.N.U (Spiritualists National Union) in the UK, serving Spiritualist Churches across the length and breadth of the North West of England and Wales.

As an SNU Medium, she has a broad outlook on faith, and the Spiritualist Churches that she serves, welcome all people of faiths, who visit to gain evidence of survival of loved ones.

She has been performing Soul Rescue for beyond a decade and has provided sessions on Energy Matters at Manchester College of Arts and Technology. An Energy Healer since the 80's she taught Therapeutic Touch to Nurses and Therapists at Manchesters' world renowned Wythenshawe Hospital. During her latter years as a Senior Nurse Night Manager at Wythenshawe Hospital, Penny regularly buoyed up the night staff with Healing and Messages from their Spirit Helpers. A Nurse, Chartered Purchaser, retired Football Referee, Teacher of Further Education and finally (and perhaps not before time!) an Author. Penny regularly speaks on Energy Matters and has finally made that great and important step, to share her wisdom, experience and know how, with her fellow earth dwellers.

Spirit Writers

The writer is joined in some chapters, by her spirit writer companions. Read their pronouncements on what is uniquely satisfying work for anyone with a big enough heart to carry it out.

Personal protection

To assist you with the discipline required to stay even-minded, uplifted and permanently optimistic, Penny has included the basic cleansing and re-energising visualisations which she uses every day in her work as a Medium and healer.

Energy Field care

For the benefit of the 'sensitive' amongst you, there is good sound advice about care of the HEF (Human Energy Field) to increase your daily quality of life and keep you a positive big soul!

Templates

Finally, there are two templates to assist you in your work. The first is a copy of Penny's letter of introduction to Landlords and Estate Agents, detailing recent legal cases with buildings found to be haunted or stigmatised. This will be of use should you wish to work to provide a service on this more formal footing. In the business sense, you will benefit from noticing how many aspects of the work need to be included in your letter of approach.

The second 'template' is contained within the chapter on how to resolve a haunting. Every consideration is included to assist you in your work.

The Author advises that anyone embarking upon resolving hauntings should be responsible enough to know themselves to have good physical and mental health.

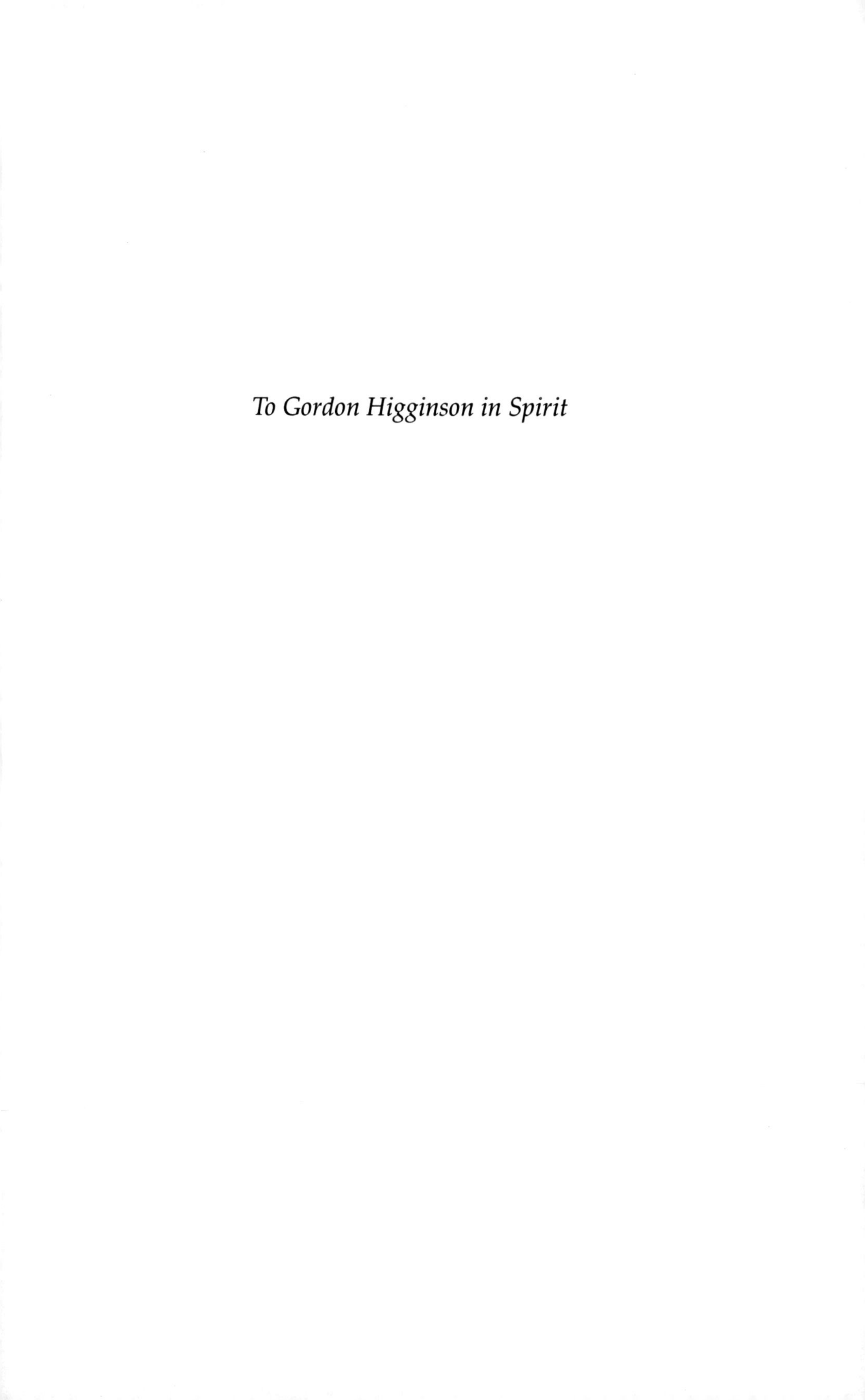

To Gordon Higginson in Spirit

Acknowledgements

WE AS humans tend **not** to see problems, wrong decisions and any subsequent slowing down of ambitions, as a positive factor in our individual lives. I wish to publicly acknowledge all those things in my life, as bringing me to this point in my personal growth, which is described by Ramadahn—through the Mediumship of Ursula Roberts—as the CONTRIBUTION stage.

This stage occurs in all our lives. So, here I am at mine, giving first hand wisdom and experience of resolving Hauntings, by rescuing souls.

I'd like to thank the late Dr Leslie Doyle, so memorable a Chest Physician that a Ward at the Wythenshawe Hospital in Manchester, England, bears his name. He demonstrated to me that, knowledge and vast experience can be lost to the masses at death. Although he actively passed on learning, not least by his extraordinary recall of details of cases and papers, there was an immense loss of mentally held data which science has yet failed to find a way to download!

For all nurses, wherever they may be, for they regularly heal and perform soul rescue, when carrying out the nursing duty of 'Last Offices'.

Finally, to those eminently wise souls who have helped me, supported and taught me, whatever I have been doing. All of them working from the Spirit realms, downloading their expertise as required; Teachers, Healers, Philosophers, Guardians of Souls and Workers for Spiritualism.

Prologue

IT'S JANUARY the 1st 2009 and I'm just putting the finishing touches to my first real book. I'm in harmony with my life's' purpose (I hope) but on reflection, January 1st 2008 found me in a similar position. However, the lessons and changes that brought me to this point one year later have changed my life forever!

I was completing my research on *Haunted and Stigmatised Buildings,* working into the night, searching out *'decided cases'* that only seemed to exist outside the UK; in the USA (where else) and New South Wales (hmm..)

Fired up with a recent experience brought to my attention, of a single mum renting a very *active* house, I was now intent on organising a research based article for Landlords and Housing Associations. The young mother had carpeted her house with hard come by money and wasn't too willing to leave (why should she?). The house was inhabited by stubborn, tenacious astral dwellers and this hadn't happened overnight.

The question that frustrated me was why hadn't the Local Council Offices been made aware of the problems before moving her in? Had they been made aware and simply disregarded tenant feedback? The phenomena were so assorted; they simply had to have existed a long, long time. There is a growing tendency to rent these days and turnover of occupancy is quicker than in the past. We have to consider therefore, that there is less history available of past tenants due to shorter occupancy periods, and who knows how they conducted their lives behind closed doors?

Firing up my laptop on 1/1/2008, I produced a paper entitled *LET THE BUYER BE SCARED? The Rights and Responsibilities in Managing the Problem of Haunted & Stigmatised Buildings, during the Transfer of Occupation by Sale or by Let.*

I then wrote out to Estate & Rental Agents, to suggest to them why they had a responsibility to potential occupiers and, how I could assist them with this and some listened! Work and referrals now come from all directions and I know that if there is a situation that will stretch me, teach me or simply needs me, Spirit helpers will send me there. An aim whilst writing this book is to illustrate how souls think and act, when earthbound, their limitations and their power to rationalise as intelligent entities. So enjoy and maybe do a little or a lot yourself when the opportunity is given, because I'm going to show you how!

Penny Barber

Chapter 1

The Human Soul

LETS GO back to the beginning, to when you were simply a twinkle in someone's' eye.

You made the decision to come to this Earth, this physical state, and your intended host on the Earth decided to have a baby.

Many conditions had to be met, authors specify a range of these, some linked to Religions, Karmic and Astrological influences, to name but a few, but lets 'kiss' this and keep it simple. Your entry into this world, barring the odd human error on the way, was made under conditions perfect to you. Everyone is born equal and whether you feel you are 'less than', due to height, weight, creed, gender, physical or mental weakness or genetic make-up, or even geographical location, then for the purpose of this book, you have survived. You have coped, lived and inevitably will return your physical body to the nitrogenous shared earth of mankind! Personally I prefer Cremation and I'll explain this in a later chapter.

You, as a spirit hovered around your mother and when the going looked good, you descended into the womb, joined the foetus and a quickening (movement) was felt by your mother.

You became a soul, encasing your little body and then you were born, at which point your spirit body or aura, started to define you, taking in sights and sounds, taking energy from the universe, to balance energies to every part of the growing body. You hopefully absorbed huge amounts of love from those who doted on you and your physical body was nurtured by milk products and, in good time, food from the good earth.

You had, as part of your structure—and always will have—a spirit body which is a fine matrix of lines of energy, moulding the very cell structure of your body and storing every happening, good and not so good. We are energy, and we use our creativeness whilst on the earth, to master the levels of earthly existence. These levels or Planes of existence are of Physical, Mental and Emotional concerns. When we come to the end of our physical lives, that soul is set free. We can then aspire to join our forebears in the world of spirit (heaven) This journey is one where we need the lightest of touches from spirit, to guide us on our way. Often family will attend from spirit world, to help us make that transitional leap. The leap is to leave behind the physical body, readjust to the omnipresent spirit/soul body and to discard unnecessary material links with the earth's atmosphere.

So, cremation or any form of death by burning, quickly releases the souls physical energies previously required for the earths' atmosphere. Burial and enfoldment by water (ie drowning) can, in some cases, tie the unenlightened to the grave a little bit longer.

You can still love, you can still think in human terms, you can still assist those left behind, it takes time according to earth customs, to move further still. My maternal grandmother has communicated with me and helped me for the past last 50 yrs, since she made her physical transition in 1959.

To avoid any delay with this process of moving to lighter spheres, you can help another's progress when you hear of a passing, no matter who it is:—

Sincerely ask that they are guided to the light.

Ask for loved ones in spirit to come close and rekindle old friendships

Ask for healing to be administered along the way.

This will make my job a lot easier, so thanks in advance to all of you putting this into practice. I always say, that when my time comes, if I can, I will ask "that my guardian guide me to the light". This is a simple mantra, but great to have in your understanding for the future inevitable!

Chapter 2

Misconceptions of Death

IF WE all had a perfect understanding of the process of transition from this physical plane, then we would possibly be a happier bunch of little humans. We wouldn't fear failure; we would make brave victims of violence or torture - if ever the need arose. We wouldn't fear aging but would wear our older bodies as a badge of experience. We wouldn't fear disease and its consequences, for we would welcome the next chapter in our onward journey. It's a fact that we fear physical death (or its mode) yet it is the most natural and advantageous state to enter. We, as mortals, simply find it difficult to visualise immortality.

Grief is the inevitable, so even with true faith and trust in the survival of the human soul, we will continue to grieve for a loved ones' passing, for they leave behind an emptiness in our energy fields, where their words of love, their smiles, joint experiences and their physical presence, can no longer be heard or seen. When we lose a loved one to physical death, part of us dies. Shared energy dies, heart strings have nowhere to entwine themselves, no physical home, part of our auric field is shocked and directionless. This is a shared energy, built up often over a lifetime. Grief hurts, lasts and affects us physically. The definition of a love heart is two auric fields intertwining. Following the death of one person, just cut the love heart down the centre and remove a half, and see how much existence is lost. How long do we sympathise with the grieving for, a month? 3 months? Try 3 years.

Bring back black arm bands!

A human in grief, is a very special and fragile member of society.

There can be barriers to incomplete soul transition, beliefs being one of them and can hinder us. In Soul Rescue, you starkly experience how our beliefs on the Earth, can colour our 'ascent' into the higher realms, even to the point of blocking the actual process. When we are dealing with the 'earthbound' soul population, we find a mix of reasons for them not reaching the heavenly realms. So whether it is their personal understanding of what death should have felt like (and didn't), their belief that they are still alive, or a real fear that they will end up in hell, it obviously and actively did delay their transition!

So if concerned at having a mixed reception on arrival, then comfort yourself by knowing that:—

1. Most of what you have done on earth should be put down to experiencing, if you are in the habit of judging yourself.
2. If you have addressed your main failures before lift off, then it will be recognised in advance of your journey.
3. The process of putting things right in spirit realms, involves some highly satisfactory work of your choosing and definitely doesn't involve shovelling coal into a furnace (if you get my meaning)

So those in the halfway house of the astral plane are doing themselves an injustice and to add insult to injury, so to speak, unwittingly annoying a number of innocent house dwellers at the same time. The Earthbound also have an annoying habit of attaching their needs to a relatively small number of us who are displaying a similar dependency, mood or weakness. There is no doubt that there will be an attachment of sorts, made with, for example, alcoholics, obsessive's and drug users, as they can retain their craving for drugs etc. I have undertaken a number of such 'exorcisms', included later in this book.

Chapter 3

The Astral, what it's like to be stuck there and, why it's not an option

SPIRIT GAVE me the following definition of being earthbound: *A being, having made an incomplete transition to higher vibrations, finds themselves enacting a fixed physical existence in a moving earthly time frame, thereby enduring a lonely and uninspired life.*

Many readers will have an understanding of the astral plane of existence. It bridges spirit and physical realms and links with the heart Chakra.

It is a super highway that we all do share (hence some very odd dreams) and it is the meeting place for us and our loved ones in dream state—a compatible place. Most times we do not remember this lovely meeting, sometimes we do. So, you could say we go back to heaven at night.

To define an earthbound soul, it should be understood at the outset, that there is a physical death process which can be halted a few days or for a longer period of Earth Time. Time as we know it here, is relative to how we experience it here and mercifully, this is not the case on the Astral Plane.

The move from life to 'death' is so simple and natural, that many, who have passed, are for a time unaware of it having happened. It might in some cases be only when the individual hears prayers and thoughts being given for their passing, that the realisation is made clear to them!

So in this book we are dealing with, in the main, earthbound souls who, over time, have failed to find their mark for one reason or another. Just as we need to ground ourselves in the magnetic energies of the earth, to live, respond to life and prosper, rather than attempt to float through life without foundation, so the 'earthbound souls' need to do just the opposite. They need to direct their energies at leaving the magnetic plane and all its momentary hardship, deciding that they are 'good already' and so move into that love supported atmosphere of the highest and best vibration, the higher realms, heaven.

An example of this occurred about two years ago and is relatively common in my work. I called to have a friend's dog clipped at a local groomers. As she made conversation, I had a strong feeling of gloom around the whole of the ground floor of the building, we somehow got onto the subject of my work and she pointed to the local business directory on the counter, stating that she had my number and was soon to call me to resolve a haunting. I mentioned the low emotion I was picking up and she immediately described similar feelings about the first floor living premises. She had dreamed of moving into the flat above her salon, but felt uncomfortable and distressed about the move. I identified the presence of an elderly couple, who also had worked the premises as a shop, post war. I was encouraged by the present owner, to find out why they appeared hostile to her, and so I spent some time, chatting with them about the effect they were having on the lady. They were 'mortified' to find they had done this, by not relinquishing their attachment after death. It was resolved amicably, the couple being extremely anxious to apologise for the upset this had caused. They would only leave once I had explained this fully to the owner and they gained her forgiveness. The owner moved in to the living accommodation shortly afterwards. Oh I had the dog clipped free, by the way!

How does it feel to be on the Astral? Souls have described it as lonely, unfulfilling, boring, frustrating, giving a selfish account of the effect the mortals are having on their existence.

If you look at the work of Carl A. Wickland MD, in the 1920s there are many accounts of the souls, through the trance Mediumship of Mrs Wickland, that bear out my findings. Dr. Wickland and his wife operated what we would call today a rescue circle.

In desperation, a certain Mrs F.W. had approached the group for help. Wickland describes the case of her deceased husband, Mr F W, who was a materialist and a fatalist, believing that death was the end. He constantly told his wife that if she died, he would commit suicide. He however died first, but remained earthbound to try to convince his wife to join him (I kid you not). He was brought through to the circle by Mrs Wickland in trance, and matters were resolved. Further information given in time, related that Mr F.W. was recruited into a team of ministering spirits whose' job it is, even in today's' world, to encourage the earthbound to move on, by descending into the astral level to help.

So, the astral is a very busy superhighway of visiting souls & visiting helpers, shared emotions and thoughts and, some unfortunates who have loaded their etheric bodies with alcohol, drugs, or the heavier passions of living, sufficient to keep them rather stuck. Those who keep themselves away from the light because of misguided beliefs are also added to these, as are those who, for a time at least, do not realise that they have lost their mortal bodies!

Recently I was called to a very 'active' larger terraced house in Liverpool. I was asked, by the nervous wife who had personally called me in, to just 'get rid of them, for pities sake get rid of them'! A spirit gentleman drew near and pointed to the fence bordering the end of the garden. On questioning, it became clear that this was her father and that he was buried just beyond the fence, in the local cemetery! The wife obviously had some sort of belief, because she said she always felt her father was near her, which was true for a number of reasons, but the point of this little anecdote, lies not in the cemetery, but in what I discovered next…

I had been given the run of the house, to resolve the problem, and came upon her husband, very much alive, playing card games on a computer screen set up in one of the bedrooms. He said, over his shoulder, 'Don't mind me luv.' just as I was just considering the futility of asking him to turn off the screen for a few minutes. Most clients recognise the reverence of this type of work and turn off music and televisions when I arrive. I had decided to try to concentrate on the work in hand, and ignore the poker screen when my attention was turned to a very strange astral sight, just behind him. As the husband was turned, facing towards his screen to my right, a male soul was sat, facing in the opposite direction, sat on a toilet, yes a TOILET.

Now consider this, its quite an enlightening position because a) it shows how the two worlds interpenetrate each other, its not a 'vertical height thing' and b) this poor soul was physically dead, did not have a body, was not eating and therefore did not need a toilet.

Chapter 4

Communities on the Astral Plane

Spirit writer

THERE IS little communication on the astral level, save a like-minded group with a thin common thread of thinking arriving and existing in the same place. The writer will now give you the benefit of her experiences, but we wish to discourage the practice of encouraging these phenomena, as it cuts across the law of existence. There is a time and a place for living, either in the physical world or, the world of Spirit.

Whereas we encourage those in visitation to loved ones and those sharing a common interest in your earthly activities, there is nothing to be gained in keeping the physically dead, near to the earth. It is a degenerative process, where once free thinking souls, become unhappy, frustrated, confused and, at the mercy of the negative energy of the fully degenerative. It is a state as unwelcome, as a physically decomposing body, unattractive, having no further practical use and, potentially hazardous to health!

Added to this, if you believe in life eternal (and you will have to sooner or later… then you will by now understand that everyone of you should have the rite of passage into a shining, fulfilling future existence. We feel that the enlightened amongst you may come to regard this as a human rights issue; after all, they are human souls needing help, not persecution.

I took a group of students to an end of terrace house, one dark and wet night. The pavements and road were black and shiny, reflecting moonlight on rain. We reached the curving narrow terraced street of 1900 housing, all aware of the feeling of moving back in time. I had received a phone call to resolve the haunting, which had become troublesome enough to produce physical effects on the young couple living in the strangely shaped, larger house at the end of this strange street. We were transfixed, as we stood looking down its curving length. Victorian children kicking tin cans, a carter, transporting casks of ale, a gentleman strolling, with cane and top hat.... All visible to the developing mediums present. Each student describing what they saw, with confirmation coming from others within the group. In this situation, individuals will 'see' spirit images their way, but a strong theme will always run through the information, as evidence that its is 'real'.

The couple welcomed us and, as we piled up our coats and umbrellas, my attention was strongly drawn to the front living room and the coal fire, but more of that a little later. The young husband had given a history of continuous sore throats, with no clear diagnosis. He had become so desperate that he had undergone a tonsillectomy, yet the sore throats persisted. They were aware of the history of the house being haunted, yet they had liked its proportions and its end of terrace position. Much as they had hoped to continue to bring it up to date with clean lines and uplifting paintwork, they were becoming increasingly aware that the building was affecting the husbands' health. His throat was more painful in an empty room upstairs. The toddler son was also unsettled in his own bedroom.

As is my requirement, we were allowed to visit every area of the building and due to the huge numbers of souls present, this was to be a longer than anticipated visit.

We worked together, the students giving evidence of what was seen. There was an overabundance of earthbound souls.

Some a little menacing because they felt vulnerable, many children were sensed, comforted and sent to the light , but we later found out that the building had been used as an early 'refuge' for the poor. In the empty upstairs room, We established the presence of a poor, ill soul who had suffered TB and throat cancer. As he lay on his simple mattress, covered by shabby blankets and coats, he was reassured of his bright journey and was thankful to move on. As we gathered finally in the sitting room below, the husband reported that his throat had lost its soreness. Everyone was elated, he sitting blissfully happy, whilst his wife excitedly went off to make hot drinks.

We were sat in front of the fires' cosy glow, probably the only coal fire to be had in the street. The young couple described their joy at finding the fireplace and turning its hearth back into a coal fire. The visiting group realised, as we sat and recounted the nights work, that the little front room was also packed with the souls of the street community of the early 1900's and it became apparent that this had become their 'favourite place' since the re-instatement of the fire. This whole community had managed, by thought, memories and need, to stay in the one same area. We organised an amnesty with them, knowing from experience that problems would persist with this level of spirit activity. They were made aware that they would meet in Heaven and could continue as a more active community there. As we left and piled into the car, we all agreed that heaven must have been rocking that night!

In a North Manchester house, the owner had a love of Victoriana and had called me in due to unexplained phenomena. I made my cursory inspection of the house, a Victorian mid terraced property.

The young owner had themed the house, true to its age, but incredibly, the front sitting room would have been a credit to a social history museum, it was amazing! I worked through the house but made a mental note to leave the 'parlour' for the final work of the visit. I had found in the main, the spirit presences were his ancestors in visitation, keen to answer his questions on 'who's who' in the photographs lining the wall. Paul had an obvious interest in them and so they had picked up on his thoughts to them, as naturally happens.

Over a cup of coffee, I started questioning him about the 'parlour,' asking did he use it to the full. He paused, and then said, I NEVER go in there. I asked why and he tried to rationalise his lack of use of this room.

I suggested that he was actively being kept out! The souls in there had managed to deter any entrance to or use of facilities, as effectively as putting a red KEEP OUT notice on the doorway.

Recounting to him the group of souls who were actively living there, I described the Victorian chaise longue sofa as having three individuals sat on it, and all souls 'in the mode of the 1900s'. With his consent, I proceeded to explain to these lodgers, the true state of affairs. They apologised grudgingly and eventually acquiesced. They were assisted in moving on.

I well remember a Spiritualist Church in a neighbouring area, asking me to take a group into a house that was heavy with negative entities. The young lady trying to take up her tenancy in the house would not stay overnight. The group of student rescuers met me and took me on a dark and shaky journey in an old car with poor suspension. I remember thinking that I probably couldn't find my way back, on foot, as we wound bumpily through an old quarter on the outskirts of Liverpool.

I went into the small terraced dwelling, with serious apprehension and yet would walk away that night, knowing that there is no fear in this work, if you operate on a love vibration. We found a motley assortment of once violent thieves, muggers and addicts who had somehow drifted into a shared combined space in the old terraced house. It took a couple of hours of 'speaking' with these poor souls and in this instance working with the Christ light that they all acknowledged from childhood teachings. When this higher being made His presence known, they realised that they were still 'children' of God and, through the love that we, as a group poured into the 'stuck souls', they showed trust and gave themselves up to the manoeuvre of being sent into the light (more of the actual manoeuvre later).

However much these souls fall into one space, it is essential in this work, that these souls are spoken to individually, as the unique and separate entities that they, like we all, are.

Due to the fact that these souls are intelligent entities, still enjoying the course vibrations of the physical, that they can, by thought vibration, tell us their hopes, fears and self-judgements, that which denies them access to Heaven. If we can't ascertain their needs, then we can't provide for them, a logical and believable account of the process of moving on and their future wellbeing, as part of the outcome of letting go. When I use the word 'believable' to describe how the soul accepts the information given at rescue, it can be likened to a 'truth' that we accept in life. The soul makes a decision that what is being said is right and acceptable to its self.

There is a more difficult community where energies combine to work to as changing phenomena, ie Shape-shifters.

Definition Of A Shape-shifter—A Shape-shifter is a collection of energies, pooled together to form a changeable shape, having a collective intelligence able to act in a collective way on a mutual course of action, formed in response to perverse human behaviour or thought, with perverse aims, thereby transgressing universal laws (Barber. P 2007).

Spirit writer

We have been asked to try to explain and rationalise this phenomena. This is a perplexing and upsetting turn of events for you to have to resolve. This type of phenomena is stubborn and cunning and yet can be dissolved by appreciating its make up. Similarly, it can be enhanced by feeding its form (as in spirit baiting for media value) The writer will explain the method in a later chapter, but it remains for us to say that these energies shouldn't be encouraged or challenged, but should be dispersed at their lowest common form.

I have been given, by spirit helpers, numerous opportunities to resolve such communities of energy. It can be done and depends on the rescuer appealing to the guardians of every source of this energy. The problem arises when the people bothered by the phenomena, start to rekindle its existence and it is this misguided action that will simply re-energise more phenomena!

Spirit baiting and troublesome spirits

I was asked the 'defining question' by a developing Medium, at Colwyn Bay Church in Wales, UK. "Penny, I thought that we all have freewill and that this impacts on whether we want to move from the Astral, into Spirit, as well." This was a great question, because we want to know just how far our freewill stretches, don't we? You could look at a parallel situation in our physical world and see that when our behaviour is not benefiting us, or hurting another, then the law of the land might well intervene.

I had been speaking to the Circle, on troublesome spirits, so going back to that defining question, my answer had to be, laying my reputation on the line, that there is a time in the existence of the individual, where their Guardian is able to intervene and make a decision on their behalf, and this is one of them.

Chapter 5

Earthbound, Residual or just visiting?

BEFORE WE look at the process of soul rescue, it's useful to identify that there is a soul to rescue! To clarify whether you are dealing with the Earthbound, and not simply residual energy or visitation, you should simply test it. Residual energy won't take a blind bit of notice of anything you do… Last year I visited a well known Welsh battlefield. As I approached the site in my car, I viewed hundreds of soldiers cutting of heads and slicing organs, doing soldierly things, yet only one approached me. He was on horseback, he was checking me out, but most of all, he was interacting with me. He was responding to stimuli, he was live energy. So when we see a legion of Roman soldiers marching through a building, just marvel and enjoy.

Spirit Writer

On the subject of residual energy, our actions and thoughts are saturated in the very buildings we inhabit, the clothes we wear and the material objects that we once held dear. The energy of history exists in another time and space and what has taken place can repeat itself as an echo of the past. Residual energy is likened to the banana skin after the feast; it does not taste of the fruit, can still mimic the shape of the fruit but is useful for neither man, nor beast.

Still on the subject of checking out residual energy, I was performing Soul Rescue in a troubled house, in an ancient Cheshire village. A cluster of modern bungalows had been built on spare ground in the 1960s and a couple were making quite major changes to their home. The troublesome male soul who was scaring the 19yr old son, was simply lost and was happy to be helped, however, the largest bedroom held a big surprise. When I saw a two housemaids circa C18 making one of the beds and not responding to stimuli I realised that another energy was sustaining this scenario. The village has at least two impressive manor houses and was known to be a well worn route for trading and merchants. Stirring up this energy was a gentleman on horseback who was taking his own shortcut across what would previously have been common land. He dismounted, bowed to me in making acquaintance and agreed to re-route in future. Nice chap, one for the ladies I sensed, no further problem, finito!

Loved ones in visitation, we will always find, whenever there is troublesome spirit activity. They tend to be related to the occupiers of domestic dwellings and are present in an uplifting and protective role. It's wonderful to perform spirit rescue and pass on messages from late family, however, its not always just family who are visiting…

I always know when the souls are visiting, because they let me know. If they are family to the occupiers, they will give names and descriptions. I give that evidence of survival to my clients and it's a sort of extra bonus to the 'settled state' of the home that they can anticipate when I have performed the work and left the building. Just like all family members, relatives beyond the veil are able to visit regularly, especially when we are sending out thoughts of love to them.

Our loved ones in spirit are ALWAYS aware of any haunting activity and come close in an attempt to resolve the problem, not, as we might expect, by having some type of spirit confrontation with the 'astral trespasser' this doesn't happen, or it doesn't work.

Cleverly, what loved ones will do, is they will cause poltergeist (noisy ghost) activity. This draws attention to the problem and eventually, help is sought.

A supreme example of this was a call I received some years ago. Jane, now in her late thirties, was experiencing orbs, in her bedroom at night. Jane had been very low since her mother had passed a couple of months ago, and was finding it hard to motivate herself each and every day. I arrived at her house one cold December evening.

As is usual, I assessed the style of the housing, and more importantly, the energies of the house, from its outside aspect. This is easy because it's a part visual and part psychic observation. However, nothing could have prepared me for the visual site that met me when I was ushered in through the front door. There were bits of walls missing, whole doors off their hinges and rooms in the process (very slow process obviously) of being stripped, in preparation for smartening up. Nothing had been overlooked, stairs, bathroom, windows, I truly had the feeling that this incomplete house could blow away, just like the house that Jack built.

I introduced myself to an assortment of relatives and girlfriends who where obviously looking forward to a personal viewing of 'most haunted' was handed a mug of tea in a dubious vessel (also with cracks and evidence of better days). As always, I was humbled and thankful for the traditional welcome of a cuppa.

To delight the youngsters, I gave them a little bit of 'clairvoyance' and then turned my attention to Jane, the mum and householder. I explained that her mother was here. I described her mother very clearly, and it became obvious to me that mother had been causing the phenomena. She was determined to have her wishes known and have herself heard. If a Medium had to be brought in to give the message, then so be it, it worked!

Mum proceeded to tell her daughter that she now felt great, that she was doing her shopping in Harrods of London, and couldn't be done for shoplifting? With that, the family exploded into laughter, Jane flung her arms round me and crying and laughing at the same time, she suddenly sat back and, getting her breath back, explained that her lovely mum had once been accused of shoplifting, because the baby buggy had hooked a small garment on its way round the store. This had become family history, but was the perfect evidence that Jane needed. I asked mum what was concerning her so much that she had to go to such lengths to have it resolved. She related that she wanted her daughter to obtain her portion of the estate, so that she could complete the work on her house. I related this to the family and Jane pointed out her sister, saying that they both badly needed the funds, yet they had felt it might seem a little grabbing, so soon after mums passing. Added to this, the third beneficiary, a brother, was comparatively well to do, living in London and didn't need the money immediately, so they were loathe to contact him on the matter. Mum became a little agitated and said, *"Do it now, you need it and the money is there for you now, just when it is needed most."* Jane and her sister promised mum that they would do her bidding and, I know that they did, because I was called back a couple of months later, simply because Jane wanted to know what mum thought of the changes. The house was really looking great. New windows were now in place, decorating was being completed and, more important than all the material changes, a radiant and focused daughter had emerged, as I saw when Jane opened the door to me.

Some 'visitors' are not connected with the family, are few and far between and if they are making troublesome visits, then they will sharply move off, when spoken to. I see them literally 'pop off' like a little balloon floating off, very quick when they do it! My helpers show me very clearly, the differing scenarios. If a visiting soul is just being nosey, I know that they don't require help and I don't waste my energies. It's enough for them to know they've been seen!

Some visit for longer than they anticipated and are literally a little stuck. They cause problems because they are trying to communicate or make sense of their situation. Some will exhibit poltergeist (noisy ghost) activity in an effort to be sorted out. I visited a newer housing estate in Oldham, Lancashire. The young couple were having all sorts of problems. The husband was quite philosophical and interested, whilst the poor wife jumped at every observance that I made, to the point where I wondered whether I was doing her more harm than good! The problem is that the haunting is simply never going to go away, so I tend to stay with my intention of rescue, despite such circumstances. If you get a difficult situation, you have either got to inject a bit of humour, or illustrate to the tenant, what an unhappy situation it is for the poor soul involved. I always emphasise that once they are moved on, then the likelihood of a return is rare.

Anyway, in this particular rather complex haunting, I spied a gentleman sitting in their bay window, wearing a hooped jersey in distinctive colours. He was staring out over the lawns in front and, when I asked the couple whether they recognised him, the husband (ex rugby player) said no, but those were Oldham's' old rugby jersey colours, and that the estate was built on the old Oldham Rugby Ground the turf of which was in that very same direction of the bay window view. He further informed me that many were the 'ashes' scattered on that hallowed turf… hmm.

When I get to these types of hauntings they are quick to resolve, but there was more to come, during my visit.

Some souls are elderly and confused and simply need a helping hand, yet, this is the exception rather than the rule with the passing of the elderly. Most elderly people making their transition, have the wisdom, grace and understanding, built up over a long lifetime, to pass eagerly into the arms of loved ones who meet and guide them, coupled with the fact that the lighter vibrations of the elderly body make it difficult for them to remain with ease in the earthly spheres. I suppose it's the ratio of deaths due to ageing, that presents rescuers with a higher incidence involving this age group, but they only need slight nudging!

So if I mention to you that the Oldham house was in close proximity to two Elderly Peoples Homes, you will appreciate that when I found a couple of oldies who had lost their way to Eternal Rest, I wasn't surprised. Our old friends had obviously found themselves being attracted to the spirit activity at our long suffering couples' house. One of the two was a gentleman, an old soldier, according to the medals on his jacket. True to form, this polite, elderly gentleman was hovering just inside the hallway. He was a strong presence and his thoughts were a mixture of "I don't wish to intrude any further because I think I'm in another's home"and "I'm a soldier and will show strength in the face of the unknown." Now, you will just have to imagine the effect of these mixed feelings, on the unfortunate young couple! In effect, when they entered the house, they had a reluctant visitor on what amounted to guard duty!

The above adequately illustrates the need to take a written history, the breadth of questions that you should ask, and the answers you must record, when undertaking Soul Rescue.

So… some will visit, some will leave only residual memories being played like an old video/DVD and some will require to be helped.

Of the Earthbound, Some will be downright scared to move on. They will be scared that they are going to hell (no such place except where they are right now) due to activities undertaken whilst in the physical state. It is these that I have the greatest love and compassion for. The explanations to them have to be of necessity, long and honest, by me. I will explain to them that they will be supported by helpers in Spirit, that they should be open-hearted and open minded during the final part of their journey. We have to work on a love vibration, and even the most hardened criminal, sadist, drug runner or killer tunes in to this, knowing that we are no threat to them. They will listen, rationalise their situation and make a decision based on what they feel is the truth.

In order to both recap and prepare for the next part of this book, let us just bullet a few Soul facts:-

1. The human soul is part spirit and for the duration of its earthly journey, part human.
2. The soul, once engineered, is indestructible and can progress personally through eternity, once it has reached the correct vibration (spirit level of heaven), just as it progressed personally through its earthly life.
3. Having encountered partnerships and marriages, produced children or not, been born with a silver spoon or an addicted parent, the soul has its own unique agenda. There may have been physical or mental weaknesses, oppression by other individuals or country of origin, or simply poor decisions made on the mortal journey, all to name but a few blessings or learning experiences, but *the soul that re-*enters heaven is much wiser than that which arrived here. That realm of spirit is what it says, a home for the spirit self, a supportive and loving dimension in which to be nurtured and to progress.
4. Conversely, Earthbound souls require to be released from an existence that is a source of discomfort and fear to them, and to those affected by their activities.
5. To leave a situation without intervention, will result in increased activity, drawing other energies inadvertently into the melee.
6. To intervene and rescue can be the single, most important action you perform for a fellow soul, and you will be rewarded in the hereafter.

7. We are energy, energy is indestructible, we are intelligent energy and we communicate by thought. The ability to continue to communicate by thought, following death in the physical, allows the rescuer and the trapped soul to have a decent chat about the next step and mutually conclude on how to go forward.

Chapter 6

Successful transitions—
have a good one yourself!

Spirit Writer

WE HAVE spoken about the problems with Earthbound Souls, which, on the face of it can be quite fascinating to some of you, but, put yourself in their position, we promise you, it's unhappy and lonely an experience. Yet, we on this side of the veil do not expect, certainly any of you who reading this book, to have a problem.

However, to understand the transition process, will result in making you more aware of your own inevitable time, a glorious time and sometime into the future. You may find it difficult at present to absorb the idea, so let us have a little dummy run, ready?

One moment you will feel the encumbrances of the physical body, its weight, possibly any associated discomfort (no pain at death). Possibly accompanying thoughts, ever present worries, material needs, in fact an assortment of earth based situations. It's important for you to face the fact that on a day to day basis, only those of you with existing, life threatening illness will have the luxury of preparation.

So, wherever you may be, you will be going about your lives, doing human 'stuff'.

That in itself puts forward the first principle of the ideal passing, ie. Treat every day as though it were your last. Don't wish any day away, love your nearest and dearest, respect the greater family of man and never fear tomorrow, only respect it, yes?

Now, since we're generally unsure as to the date of our passing, it may be a wise idea to tie up a few loose ends, such as returning a book, contacting old friends, repaying outstanding 'debts' and perhaps asking us, your helpers to balance up any past poor decision making (just put out the thought if you're unsure who can help).

We will assist you in making recompense where possible, for issues you handled unwisely during your life so far. This is not a penance, please know that when you come back home to our world, we will help you to put things right in great, positive ways that will astound you in their wisdom.

So, whilst on the earth, we will put you in someone elses' life path, however briefly, just to assist them and so cancel your worries.

Your lovely soul will instinctively accept karma (rebalance) whilst on your Earth, because you have consciously accepted that there is more that you could rebalance, giving us a great opportunity to help others on your side of life.

By your tacit commitment to be of use to others during your lifetime, in all sorts of ways, you are truly doing spirits work.

So! You are now perhaps wondering how this piece of the puzzle fits…

To have an ideal passing, it is helpful to have an understanding of the position you can reach on the other side. If you recognise that we are all in this together, and that you can be of help on Earth, whilst purifying your energy field and soul combined, well, the result is that you gain an energy vibration of a higher frequency. It is that, which we in spirit associate with that which is our energy frequency as well. So you can now resonate with us!

So being mindful of your souls need to gather more love of its human vehicle (so that you can love yourself) and love from others too, you start to emanate a peace and a harmonious countenance, that helps you to trust life itself. Your self esteem of course improves, as does decision making and, because we are consciously working along side you, then your trust in LIFE, your spirit helpers and the Angelic realm, is optimised.

You no longer have a short sighted view of existence, where stress, survival and fear of failure, incite the mind to make you miserable.

Life starts to flow you, as you dance to its rhythm. Life provides for you and, your Spirit self is now stronger than your Mind and Body. Your Spirit Self is now in the ascendancy and you are blending and already working with us, we who you will meet you at your transition, for, transition to Spirit world is as simple as that!

Now, lets get back to how you will feel, well, no different really, no aches and pains. Emotions are also buffered, for in the higher levels of vibration, there is only the emotion of love, like a great steam engine, it is the fuel of everything. You will feel a tremendous peace, stillness at first, to help you to re-adjust. You will be shown familiar and welcome scenes, a hospital, if your frail body has weakened your spirit, and a loved one to greet you and visit you whilst you are healing.

You will spend time reacquainting with loved ones. They will accompany you to your funeral and any inquests on the earth, and, if need be, to any associated legal sittings, if others are charged with your demise. They, your loved ones and helpers, will help you to acclimatise. They will help you to adjust to use your powers of thought in reaching people and places. Thought is now your vehicle for movement so that you may spend sometime visiting far away places, perhaps the Rocky Mountains, or other natural wonders. There will always be the opportunity to use any such forays, as a time of reflection, to help you to relinquish the physical life.

When you are ready, in time, you will be taken to a place for you alone, with sustenance to hand should you need it, and in the solitude of that time, you will review your life's' story. As a result, you will know just where your efforts must lie, in making recompense, and this work will be exciting and exacting.

As we work and communicate by thought, you will be in touch with loved ones also in spirit "at a thought", so that when you are taken up with other "Labours of Love", then you release their time with you, so that they may do likewise.

There is time given to old and new leisure pursuits, favourite social events, music, discussion, plays, dance, reading, and learning new skills as wished. All this for as long as it suits you. Eventually you will leave the comfort zone of the familiar, to soar to the heights of combined and multidimensional thinking, but not until you are ready in your 'self.'

Just as you will also try to communicate with those left on Earth, to help on what ever level you choose, so we hope now, that by this communication, we have reached, helped and resonated with you as this chapter concludes.

Yours in love and understanding,

Ramadhan

Chapter 7

How to help others in their transition

Spirit Writer

WE HAVE spoken of how important the individuals' stance on death is, yet not all will have probed this area of existence, many expecting that death is all there is and nothing lies beyond it.

With that mindset, there is bound to be momentary confusion, principally because when that person passes, they will feel that they haven't, and may well have to rely on thought transmission from their nearest, speaking such words as "John has died" or "Johns' funeral is next Thursday". We, in Spirit, will always know of a passing and will work to bring the deceased's' consciousness into a compatible state with ours.

Many will be made aware of loved ones coming close, and will gladly follow them as a rear Guard action, as they are shown the light of spirit. Those living to a great age, having outlived many of their family, will pass this way, their mindset being of a simple belief that all will meet up again.

Those passing unexpectedly through trauma, will always be met and taken away from the scene, by someone they feel immediate trust in, so that they needn't witness the aftermath. They are moved to a familiar scene, perhaps a café, or a hospital waiting room, to have things gently explained.

There are relatively few souls requiring rescue, and there is no penalty in cases of suicide, addiction or murder. As we have mentioned, it is the mindset at the time of passing, that is responsible for the pace of full transition. When you hear of a suicide, wish them well, for their pain and learning is in the grief they leave behind.

In your uniqueness, you deal with both your life and death in your own way, yet have compassion and thoughts for the newly passed, because you can't judge their needs or limitations beyond your world. In doing this, you are performing soul rescue in a fundamental way.

This brings us to the question of murderers and sadistic bullies, rapists and torturers. They are cocooned in a place of safety, enshrouded by their energy field memories of every deed they have committed against another human soul. Just as we are encouraging you into right thinking by trust and self esteem, so that your energy is light and lovely, so imagine what they have brought into our world. They are kept in the depths of their thinking and it is almost a catch 22 situation as you call it. We have workers here who will try to pierce the gloom of their existence, to those who are trapped in replaying their worst atrocities. The energies will start to change, the moment they can express the thought of compassion for their victims. This has the effect of bringing the light of love vibrations into their cocoon. It is this single thought that must replace their thoughts of fear for self. The need for self preservation and then, the self loathing that they will experience, are part of the gradual process for self realisation and self assessment to complete.

The ministering souls then will work with the darkened soul, to rehabilitate them in ways, unique to their needs. They then have to work to have the shackles of their human memories, removed without eventual trace.

Chapter 8

Spirits' support promised, to soul rescuers

Spirit Writer

WHEN YOU embark on soul rescue, you will encounter many different scenarios, and similarly, you will continue to encounter situations that you have prior experience of. We ask you to trust your faculties in the early years and know that we recognise your strengths and limits of experience and of course, we will actively help you.

We will give you the easier situations first and gradually ease you into the more complex. Before making a decision to embark on this dedicated work, please know that we welcome you with open arms, that we will guide and protect you and, open up to you the realisation that you will always be working with THE LIGHT, on a love vibration. You will never have to endure the darkness that these poor souls have to suffer. You will be a light, shining in their dark corner. They will feel your love and see your light and, be guided to you, as you in turn will be guided to them.

We know ***all*** *our band of soul rescuers (here the writer has to pause as overwhelming emotions of love engulf her); we know where you are and when you can be available. We will use your skills and good intentions, teaching you by the task that we place in front of you. Already, as you realise that you will be precious to us, we are* *providing helpers and teachers for you. They will work in your aura, to direct and protect you. The writer of this book enlists, amongst others, the Angelic Realm, as part of the workforce. It is essential that a team is formed from both sides of the veil; you are the physical embodiment of our spirit enterprise!*

We suggest that you call upon us with your fears and apprehensions, before each encounter and, we will let you know there and then, that your needs will be met. Please remember that your needs are met already, but it is good to pray and voice your concerns, because in doing so, you demonstrate your belief that a higher power than yourself alone, is required to complete this work. It is a privilege on both sides, to work towards such a mutual aim.

Should you take up the work, then welcome and thank you, friends.

Ramadhan

In the 1990s' I stood on the corner of two roads in the centre of my local Cheshire town and confirmed with Spirit, that it was time to start using my natural gifts more overtly. I was in an unhappy place in life and knew that my soul was fighting back, in order to move forward spiritually. My life was literally turned upside down, even to the point of my work changing from day shifts in nursing to permanent night duty. Spirit had obviously taken me at my word. I quickly became a certified healer and worked towards platform Mediumship, which is the calling that I love dearly.

The point I am making in this, is that I had to start somewhere, that I didn't just become a recognised 'Competent' in my work. What happened to me was that Spirit listened and gave me my dream. It took until writing this book, that I suddenly realised why I remembered the precise place where I made my wish; it was, literally, at a crossroads. They will give you your dream, your opportunity; simply make them strongly aware of the path you wish to take. How long this will take, depends on how much change is required in your thinking, your circumstances and of course, your existing skills and knowledge. So if the first point of your journey in wishing to perform soul rescue is just that, ie. 'wishing' well simply do it...... wish it to Spirit.

On a practical note, it may be that you are 'encouraged' to join a group of paranormal experts or a rescue circle. There will be much to learn and, some to discard. As you grow in wisdom, you will gain an understanding of how you, yourself, uniquely work. Take every opportunity to compare 'findings' during any group work you undertake, because this above all else will reassure you in the given circumstances and overall, will give you confidence to trust and work with your 'self.'

Chapter 9

How to resolve a haunting (soul rescue)

IT IS too easy for souls to stay around memories for too long. They do influence the energies and atmosphere of a building or place just as happened with the Dog Clippers' premises, mentioned in an earlier chapter. The better situation is for souls to visit for short periods and then to return to their current work and development in the spirit realms. This situation is nicely compatible with both realms. Our loved ones will be nudged to visit when we think about them, but generally, we will have long periods where we are more concerned with our human world. Our work, family responsibilities, pleasure or leisure, all make calls on our time, so that even though we feel we are calling on them too often, it is far from the real state of affairs. Life is definitely balanced on both sides of the veil.

They work on thought 'vibrations' in spirit world. That is because they don't have the physical organs. In the physical world, however, this mode of communication remains compatible because spirit can hear our thoughts as well! So, we can communicate and some more clearly than others. It stands to reason therefore, that we can communicate very easily with earthbound souls because they often feel they are still physical and they are most definitely present when phenomena presents ie. Their presence is made known to us.

Another important point to make, a fact for you to share with anyone interested, is that ghosts, earthbound souls - call them what you will - must be sent to the higher planes. There are many reasons to give for this, but I have named three major considerations.

1. If you read the work of Wickland C A MD. Who wrote his classic "Thirty Years Among The Dead" in 1924, you will see how alone, how confused, how weary and scared are these poor souls in the dark. An example is when Dr Wickland recounts the case of a morphine addict, craving all the time for more, whilst on the astral.
2. In the realms of spirit, there is the opportunity for the continuous growth and development of the human soul. We must allow every soul their right and this rite of passage.
3. If you leave the situation unresolved, there is no doubt that it will get worse. I have worked in this field for twelve years and have seen the consequences of inaction. In America, it is law in some states to have to admit to a building being haunted or stigmatized by tragic events, with 'decided cases' in court. The presence of earthbound spirits is distressing for the living and the dead and, is not compatible with either world.

At the outset, it is vital to mention that although the original source of the phenomena will in most cases not be known to the affected people, there are clear cases where a loved one has returned specifically to give a message. I have attended a haunting only to find that someone has called to say they love them, or please forgive them, or 'spend that money I left you', as mentioned in a previous chapter.

More generally, loved ones will use Mediums, Sensitives and Psychics, to get a message across, but from time to time, a loved one may be trying direct methods and in the process coming too close.

And this in itself may increase spirit activity, or for a brief time, make the recipient quite open to psychic forces due to the increase in magnetic energies around them. There are great lengths to which spirit may go, maybe appearing as an Orb or getting themselves superimposed on a photograph, just to say hiya!

I have already spoken of how spirit activity will increase if a situation is left too long. I **always** find that your spirit family will come around a scary situation to offer support. I often find that spirit children will muck in as well, if just attracted by the increased activity. So… working out who is who and what's what, is fundamental.

Recently, I attended a client who telephoned me earlier that day, saying that her husband was starting his night shifts the next day, and the family would move out if I wasn't able to come and visit. I made a space at 10pm and whilst taking the history, the family revealed that they had lived with the phenomena for 5 yrs. admittedly a drop in the ocean of time, to the astral dwellers under the same roof, but it had given the building time to accrue an extended astral family! As I picked my way through the souls present, there appeared a little girl of about five or six years of age, with dark hair in long, fine pigtails and a smocked dress. She was carrying a dolly, which she offered to me to hold, to take a look at. I thanked her and suggested it was time to return home, at which point a nun came forward for her, admonished her rather kindly, and off they went back to the higher realms. The main astral character, affecting the family, was a naked gentleman who I espied hiding in the chimney breast alcove. He was, I would guess, around forty-five years old, with a solid, big boned body, not fat and totally and utterly dazed but compliant. He did not know where he was. Earlier that day, whilst taking the telephone call by car phone, I had already mentally connected with him and, on finishing the telephone call, I took some time to calm his fears. I had pulled in from the road, to take this call and I stayed there to capitalise on the fact that I had his attention. I had managed to explain to him, some seven hours before the visit, what he would encounter. It was only when I reflected on how relaxed and compliant he was that night, how utterly he had placed himself in my care, that I realised that he had been given sufficient truths, to make the decision to become ultimately submissive in the actions taken to help him.

If you have a desire to help resolve a haunting, it is one of the finest services you can offer both to another soul and to their folk in spirit world. You place them back in society, back home and, onto their onward path.

If you help just one soul to the light, you have performed a charitable act that ultimately allows the earthbound soul to continue their journey, resolve their past issues and to progress to higher spheres.

There are though, many accounts captured on the media of Television, where souls are being baited and tested about their earthbound state. I was called in to help a man who had told a strong entity to clear off and that he (the man) wasn't scared of the spirit and was stronger than 'it' ever would be. The spirit bided his time for one week, waiting for the man to go take his annual holiday. From the first hour of the holiday, the spirit sang in the mans head unabatedly. From the moment the man awoke, the spirit sang internally and to make matters worse, turned the volume up at meal times to turn the poor chap off his food. The song was "The rhythm is gonna getcha, the rhythm is gonna getcha"

The lesson here is that all rescues and communication with spirit, whether trapped or just visiting, should be performed with love and understanding and on a positive vibration in thought. The Earthbound are simply that, floundering in a dark and lonely place where no-one is listening to them, no-one is attempting to establish the fears and needs of these poor souls. It may be that they fear going to Hell, due to their conduct in life - they won't! The message I give them is that they will be taken into heaven, where they will spend sometime examining their life and deciding how they can help those on Earth. I personally feel that the spirit in this true story had more freedom than most. He had attached himself to the mans energy field!

Do make the decision to speak to them as equals, which involves a respectful attitude. They must be treated as a human being, with all the foibles, fears and beliefs that you and I currently have too. I treat all souls with respect and I listen to their responses, in order to gain their trust and be allowed to help them. You may wish to speak silently to them, through the common language of thought, you may wish to include others present in the conversation. Having others present also increases the energy available to help them move to the spirit realms. It doesn't always fit the circumstance however. In a recent case, I was due to sit with a lady one afternoon, and when she arrived, it became obvious that she wished to cut a communication, rather than have one! Patricia launched into her 'horrendous' problem, whereby every night when she climbed into bed, she felt the presence of a male, keen to get physically close to her. We arranged an urgent visit and Patricia accompanied me into the Master Bedroom, just off the first floor landing, leaving her perplexed husband downstairs. I quickly located the soul, who sat on Patricia's side of the bed. He motioned for me to join him and I realised that I couldn't recount the proceedings to her, as the very thought that he was taking such liberties, would seriously upset her. I realised that he was not only similar in looks to her husband, but that he appeared of similar age too! Just as I was starting to consider a Shape-shifter type of phenomena, the man showed me a tattoo on his left forearm. He had obviously read my thoughts, and showed me that there were differences between him and her husband, and that he wasn't 'cloning' the husband. I verified the absence of tattoos, by asking Patricia about her husband arms and with that evidence, I was happy to listen to the soul's account of happenings. I sat beside him and he told me of the sort of guy he was, a hard worker who had passed to spirit with a cardiac arrest. He said that he was still a red blooded male and that Patricia was available in his space. I asked him who he would like to come and take him to a place where he could be more sociable and happy. He knew what I meant and we summoned his father. So, that was the end of that…except that Patricia asked what he was like, and particularly his age. When I estimated around fifty, she looked absolutely horrified and I suddenly knew, the less I said, the better……

METHOD FOR RESCUING

Self Preparation

When you show an interest in Soul Rescue, you will be given a helper from the world of spirit. They will already be organising a series of situations that you can work on. If you have already started, they will allow more and more complex problems to come your way, over time. You in turn must acknowledge your helpers, as they will be ready to help and will be at your side. I always speak with them; ask for wisdom beyond my knowledge and the protection needed. I can state categorically, at the time of writing, that I have never felt fear when performing rescues.

I am asked whether I take attachments with me when I leave a building. This is very rare; however, if any residual attachment does occur, your helpers will alert you to this and a solution will be found, also, there is always a positive little lesson if it does occur! We **always** gain more wisdom and blessings, ultimately.

NB. ALWAYS MAKE WRITTEN NOTES, IF YOU ARE WORKING WITH AN EXPERT GROUP, YOU MAY HAVE TO MAKE NOTES BY RECALL, ONCE YOU HAVE COMPLETED THE TASK. KEEP NOTES FOR THE BEST OF REASONS, SOME OF WHICH ARE MENTIONED IN THIS BOOK.

Tenplate for Guidence

1. You will know some of the history to the problem,
2. If it's a private dwelling, you need to know whether they own or rent the property,
3. How long they have lived (or worked) there? Is there a rapid turnover of tenants?
4. Note is the building detached, semi, flats or terraced?
5. Do neighbouring properties have a quick turnover of tenants and do neighbours complain of these problems? What can neighbours tell you about the past?
6. Did a tragedy occur in the house or in the vicinity?
7. Has there been a family happening, passing or anniversary recently?
8. Who lives at the property and what ages (children included)
9. Do the children experience anything and are any of them in puberty?
10. Is anyone in the home particularly sensitive or psychic?
11. Does anyone dabble in the paranormal?
12. What phenomena has been seen, how do you feel in its presence?
13. Where and what time of day or night is the phenomena strongest?
14. Has this happened to you before?
15. How long has it been occurring?
16. What was on this land previously?
17. What is the age of the house?
18. Have you been making any changes to the house?
19. Are there any hospitals or institutions near by? E.g. Residential homes?
20. What are the attitudes, thoughts and feelings of the occupiers?

This list, and anything relative to the circumstances, should be noted on paper. Remember my visit to the ex rugby player who had bought a house on a reclaimed and famous rugby pitch. There were two Residential Homes round the corner and John reminded me that many a time, human ashes would be scattered on the pitch as a bequest!!

So, many aspects, many considerations, not least of which would be the presence of lifelong rugby fans (which there were!) and the possibility of the exceptional case where an ex-resident of the Residential Home might have lost their way back to their Spirit Home (which indeed there was!)

When you have the fundamental information surrounding the situation, you must give an explanation of what you intend to do, to those present. They will usually organise a time with you, where children are out of the way, absolutely fine & sensible. I attended a house where the mother felt that the children should be present, plus the 12-year old daughters' boyfriend. I asked who would take legal responsibility for the boy and she said that she, the mother would. This mother was 'progressive of thought' to say the least. I however, found the voice vibration of a couple of youngsters, chatting without restraint, incompatible with the work to be done, so I sent them off, out of my earshot, whilst I completed the task.

Prior to a visit, I will explain that I do not bring anything with me, no crosses, no candles, and no props. I state that I do not use commands or 'wordy' verse. I promise that I will explain what I find and give an explanation as far as possible, as to how the situation arose… When I get to the building, I mentally take note of the physical condition and any psychic sense or feelings. I also assess the occupiers, so that I can interact with them. I get them to sign and date my form and get them to state if they wish to participate. I invite them to sense what I am sensing and to assist me in the rescue as appropriate. When I get them to sign, it is a signature to state that they are fully informed, i.e. They are giving informed consent (as far as they can appreciate what spirit is!) I have to say, that in the years of working with tenants and occupiers, the only emotion experienced when they have involved themselves practically, has been one of loving emotion and joy.

The best practice in areas of dealing with the general public is to write everything down. This serves to remind you, should you be called back to persistent problems. As a long serving general nurse, I have never forgotten the rule, 'If it's not written down, you didn't do it' so its good practice to have your written checklist, the occupiers verbal response to your open questions written verbatim, and of course, your consent form. Added to this, I always leave behind a feedback questionnaire with an addressed envelope. I ask the occupiers to respond in 6 weeks and I keep my reports as a kind of reference source!

Don't go beyond your competence level, as you will gain in competence over time. There is no doubt that the more rescues you perform, the more complex cases are sent to you. I speak of Shape-shifters at a later point, but I will simply say at this point in the book, that if a rescue is complex or you feel out of your depth, contact a Spiritualist Church or phenomena expert and ask for someone to step in and help. Please don't think you are going to make matters any worse because you are unsure of what to do. It is more a matter of what you relay to the occupiers. You can allay their fears by explaining perhaps that you haven't met with this style of haunting before and that you are going to seek some advice. What I have never done is to say I'm an old hand at it, because the day I do, I'll be given a quick lesson on how I'm not! I do however tell them of my experience in this work.

Now that you appreciate the need for some groundwork in gathering as many relevant facts as possible, and importantly, in giving reassurance to those being haunted, then the rest of the work will be centred on communicating with the all souls present. When we know where they have been seen, felt or heard, we have an indicator of where to look, but it is foolhardy not to examine the whole of the building. If the building is divided into flats or is terraced, you may need to use more advanced methods, mentioned later, to resolve such issues. Again I will say that our spirit helpers know just where to start us on our missions and will afford appropriate opportunities, or provide other experts to help us.

As I mentioned earlier, not only can we communicate by thought with spirit and they with us, but when we are rescuing Earthbound souls, we can have clear communication with them because we are in the vicinity of where they are stuck.

Explain to them, having sensed their fears or uncertainty on moving on, that the dimension of Spirit is the heaven we speak of, that no-one is punished for life decisions, that they will be given some quiet time to reflect on their life and some very positive ways of making any amends needed to those left behind.

These souls may have taken their own life, succumbed to drugs, alcohol and other addictions; they may simply have passed quickly through sudden death of trauma or killing. They may have murdered, thieved, raped or bullied and are afraid to 'meet their maker'. They may just be confused or be Earthbound through a desire to cling to the physical life. I emphasise here again, that the majority of all deaths, will result in the soul entering spirit realms.

When you become clear on the nature of the problem, you can proceed to fix it. To give an example; if a previous owner in spirit doesn't like the alterations being made to the building and are making it known by their activity, they can get stuck in their thoughts and need help to move on. This is a simple and common occurrence. The action is simple, explain that you are aware of their feelings, but that they are going against the laws of existence, and are causing anxiety and mayhem. At this point you will sense their feelings about this and you can enter a dialogue aimed at reassuring them that 'heaven is a much more dynamic place. I've gotten into conversations about how boring it is, and that no-one is taking a blind bit of notice of them. I suggest they might want to get on with hobbies and join in socially, in spirit, where they will find interaction. Next, when the moment seems right, ask them who they would wish to assist them back into the higher realms. You will 'hear' who they choose and 'see' this meeting taking place. Ask what mode of travel they prefer in order to move upwards. If it's the builder of the house, they often simply choose stairs! Think about their trade in life, and it appears a logical choice.

Remember the guy I mentioned, who was trying to hug Patricia? When the time came to make that all important journey, his father had suggested an exciting ride to the light, but his son said, come on dad, let's take a walk! It's an added bonus if a second person is helping you, as I have previously stated, because although they will see different parts of the scenario, they will verify the major and some more minor points. A major bit of evidence would be the person chosen to come for them, and stating it was father, would be a good cross reference. A minor point might be one of these little gems of 'chit chat' between loved ones, such as how to travel!

I remember many cases, where the soul felt so wretched about their life, that I had to offer my 'trump card'. I work with the Angelic Realm to resolve hauntings. I know no barriers to religious beliefs and therefore due to most faiths accepting angels, then most souls react positively to them. My trump card, for example with those of Christian faith, is the Christ light. In all cases where I have called upon Jesus, then the soul has responded quickly and positively and moved on despite their despair. This happens with both practicing and non-practicing Christians. There was a study performed recently where volunteers were subjected to pain. Where a picture of the Virgin Mary (Catholic Faith) was placed in front of the subject, the pain on a scale of 1-10 was lessened. When shown a picture of a popular female from the Media however, pain scores were equivalent to normal thresholds. The point I am making is that by our faith of our childhood teachings, we retain that faith when the going gets tough!

To assist the 'climb' into 'heaven' I visualise a bright light above me and an always rewarded with a sign that it is completed successfully. The emotion is beautiful and brings closure. Job done! Give thanks to all non physical helpers.

I generally suggest that no further thought is given to the soul, to enable the energetic link to be cut.

Seriously consider your own feedback sheet and addressed envelope, to assess the effect of the rescue after 6 weeks. As well as it being a good reference source, as I mentioned earlier, it certainly helps to monitor work effectiveness and also affords a window of reflection for the client.

Repeat visits

If a repeat visit is necessary, there is always a good reason. I have learned over the years that there are many reasons for this, and more often its because of a soul left inadvertently behind, and will usually be a result of multiple problems, however, other reasons are there and I enlarge on them in the following chapter.

At this point I will say that you are performing a service and are employing time and often fuel in the process. Please allow for a return visit if needed and try to build the expense into the first visit. You can of course resolve any minor issues by distance work, if your client lives some miles away. You do find some souls will actively hide themselves during your visit, which we will also discuss in the following chapter.

I do prefer to visit in the first instance. In the odd case where activity remains, I will work over the telephone with the client. Sometimes, clients will have a psychic awakening during haunting, prior to my visit and due to the energy present. This is an involuntary release and will diminish over time, is not good for the person and I actively discourage them from watching psychics working on TV whilst it resolves.

Chapter 10

Resolving more complex hauntings

WHEREAS THE earlier chapter introduces the reader to the basics of Spirit Rescue, we now start to look further into the complexities of working in this field. It includes Attachments and Shape-shifters and recounts some of my experiences to those who may wish to learn from them. I will say at this point, Exorcism, is basically removal of attached thought forms and works though healing vibrations.

Whether its multiple haunting, Ley lines, divided houses, shape-shifters, spirit baiters, attachments or mental health problems in clients, if you decide to specialise in the field of Soul Rescue, then your spirit teachers will bring a myriad of differing scenarios, so that you will be all the wiser and more confident to competently tackle to any haunting.

To begin with, we should look at the complexities of multiple haunting and, where a shared building exists, the same action should be considered. Shared buildings include flats, divided houses and terraced rows. To give an example of this, In 2006 I visited a Manor House, divided into lots. The section I dealt with dated back 400 years, the occupiers had lived with the activity, but felt that as they were moving to a smaller home, then I might like to have a look before they handed over the keys. I took a bunch of students with me, who bore witness to what happened and what a great experience it was for them too! At this point, I must restate that I have never suffered fear, during my work and there is no reason why anyone should, no matter the magnitude of the work. If you work on a 'love vibration' it melts the hardest heart and stuck souls respond well.

If you are working in divided premises, you must work towards clearing the building. The way to do this is firstly to go through the vital personal preparations, written checklist and then, appreciate that you are now going to have to bring earthbound souls to 'the table' to you in fact! It's particularly good to have witness support, when using this method. In the Manor House, following a reconnoitre of the available rooms, we literally sat at a table. On finding that there were no extremes of feelings sensed, that no great tragedies had occurred in the vicinity I directed the students to work in the following way.

Prepare the way by calling in the Angelic realm (recognised by most religions) the Christ Light (to support Christian souls) and importantly the guardians of the earthbound souls. The presence of a soul's guardian, when you are working with an unknown quantity is vital, as you don't want to leave any soul behind. We are given freewill in our lives, until such time that we need intervention to assure our onward journey back to spirit world. Our Guardians are at this point, allowed to intervene.

Now ask for a vortex of light energy to build up within the circle of helpers. You will see or sense this.

Now give an explanation to all spirit within the building, clearly stating that that they will all enter heaven, say that those present must be lonely and bored with their current situation and that everyone is going together, so roll up and join the band! Ask the Angelic realm to search out all souls and importantly, ask the guardians of all souls present, to take those in their charge, to the edge of heaven, so that they can choose for themselves how beautiful it is. Stay, wait, note the 'spirit activity'. Your group will bear witness to souls flying up through this opening into the higher realms, attesting to the unique feelings of these escapees at the time. One student seated with us at the Manor House, at the long Jacobean table, sat open mouthed with eyes fixed on the invisible scenario. As we held a debriefing session afterwards, he recounted a scene where one soul was trying to persuade another not to go. The reluctant soul was not impacting on the progress of the other, it (male) was just enacting a personality trait for a split-second, and then off he popped into the wild blue yonder! This illustrates that you can sense the strength of personal conviction with some souls.

In this case, the owner of the house in a previous century needed strong persuasion before bowing to the likes of peasants such as us! He was found to be sat at the head of the aforementioned table. He was a foreboding figure, whose word was never questioned. He was obviously still acting as The Lord of The Manor when we came along. Needless to say, our love and support assisted them all eventually, to the light. So, job done! Give thanks…, never forget who does most of the work and it's not us. I sometimes feel like an ambulance driver. I get the soul to the door, just like a patient is taken to hospital for emergency care, and there my responsibility usually stops. I know that the onward experience for that soul energy is endless and will involve the spirit workers' continued care.

I make a nice habit of asking for the help of the Angelic Realm to ensure that all souls have been helped. This is especially important when the problem is more complex, but I always say that one never knows the true extent of a problem or potential problem. I do also ask that any building I have worked in, benefits from a sustained angelic presence. This assists occupants in feeling calm, following proceedings, and sustains pure energies during a period where the building continues to cleanse itself.

Shape shifters

The above method can also be applied with Shape shifters and they do exist. In fact I would go so far as to say they are probably having a great time masquerading in some 'known' places of haunting. Shape shifters are a collection of energies, of the basically negative kind, little pixels of energies that work as a collective energy, which can move rapidly to adopt an image ranging from 'blood' writing on a wall, to an entity so strong it can physically mark a human. This isn't sinister in that it can be resolved with ease. The problems come when they are baited (on TV) or taunted.

As I have stated and restated, if a situation is approached with love, the natural laws will prevail.

Method - Prepare yourself, reassure the occupants particularly, and take your history, with particular attention to any other attempt to resolve the problem. An occupant should be encouraged to describe any previous efforts and the outcome. Take your written history, have an attitude of love and compassion, do not be confrontational or judgemental. Consider treating the phenomena as a group of souls, for so it is, bonded together to use all its intelligence to make things happen! You are therefore asking the Guardians of all souls present, to take their individual charges to the edge of heaven, so that they can experience the magnitude of this higher realm. I will, if I feel it appropriate, suggest that the individual can make up their mind at that point, leaving freewill as an option, but it never is a problem.

When we work with these complex cases, we sometimes find that the occupier may also have been encouraging the situation. It is by no means common, but you need to keep it in your mind as a possibility until you can logically rule it out. I have been called into a house where the wife had been actively encouraging the earthbound group to perform phenomena and they responded! To give an example, when I walked into the house, I saw in my minds eye, a young man having a shower in the bathroom that was visible from the front door. I described what I had seen to the wife and she explained that I had described her grown-up son and that he had just showered before he left the house. I was being shown by the shape-shifting entity, how clever 'it' was in reproducing a scenario! She then described scenes that she had actively encouraged, where she had applauded this entity for pushing her husband into a paddling pool! Whether he had slipped and fell, or she simply wanted to be a sensationalist about it, the entity got the spotlight and the focus. When I suggested that she gave psychism a wide berth for a while, she said that she could not promise, so my response had to be that I couldn't promise resolution.

We literally pour a lot of energy into this field of work. If I diary a haunting, I ensure that it is the last work of the day. This is because we use a lot of auric energy to energise souls and help them move on. We are also working with our auric energies to simply communicate with them and, as with any form of Mediumship, it will deplete our energy levels for a short period of time. To respect both the work we do and our energies, we are entitled to ensure that we are not making unnecessary effort.

I was asked to visit a family by a gentleman pronouncing himself a psychic witch. He stated proudly that he had 'opened up' the son to psychic powers. He was a 'friend' of the family and the mum I observed was vulnerable by virtue of her low moods. The problem was resolved but I took great pleasure in insisting that the whole family closed down to psychic activities for the foreseeable future. They did much better without him.

Humankind can cause all sorts of problems to self and others. I attended a house some 25 miles away and resolved the problem with excellent evidence of the spirit loved ones being in attendance. The phenomena was caused by a neighbour who had passed some years ago and the evidence, right down to his motorbike, was attested to by the couple who were told of this by the mans neighbours. The wife had also insisted that she was visited by spirit when her husband was away. It was very important therefore, that friends and family in spirit were also allowed to set the record straight on what she said was happening and I realised that there was another problem and that my visits hadn't ended. I always give a reasonable guarantee and so the following week when I had a call to say she still had problems, I had to undertake another 50mile round trip as she was so insistent I visit. On the way, spirit said that she sits twiddling her thumbs all day and needs to get a job. She had been dabbling in matters psychic and was actively encouraging phenomena. I passed on their advice and she agreed that this was what she needed. Her husband had been present at the previous visit, so this advice couldn't have been given in front of him without an argument. I have experienced situations where clients are serial attention seekers and perpetuate the situation. They will have gone through the list of Mediums and Churches, until someone calls their bluff. Like any apprenticeship, we have to know all likely scenarios.

Performing Telephoned Rescues. Sometimes it becomes impracticable to visit, and following a history taking over the telephone, then you can link and rescue in a short space of time. It's not ideal, but it is effective in many cases

Chapter 11

How Spirit make sure you get to visit a haunted place

SOME RESCUES are organised in the formal fashion of telephoned or e-mail requests. You will in many instances, find that a little block is put in your path on the way. This is absolutely par for the course, so to speak. I fully expect a little twist to my journey to any haunting. My SatNav sometimes goes haywire, or I somehow get lost. At this point I just remind myself that it is because the earthbound souls are always aware of your coming, and a last little bit of panic or excitement seems to 'kick in'. Clients describe more active phenomenon, once the visit has been agreed!

Some rescues are organised by spirit despite us, because they make sure that you get to where you are needed to work.

In the space of two recent weeks, I have been 'sent' to two houses, in the belief that I am to give private sittings, as a Medium. The first house was on the Wales/Cheshire border. I arrived in Wales two hours early, having wrongly read and re-read my time entry in the diary. I made the decision to re-arrange the date as I would have had to wait outside, for my clients to return from their work. I arrived on my second visit, right on time and found that I was put into a room that was filled with about 20 coalminers! I sent them on to spirit in little coal trucks, then found that I couldn't work to provide an effective sitting that night because I had used my energies elsewhere. The whole scenario was exceptional and unusual, but if you live magically, then you accept and marvel at life on both sides of the veil. I can see however, why I wasn't invited for a return visit. The Welsh/Cheshire border provided the venue for the second event as well. I agreed to call to give a private sitting to a young mum, on my way back from Chester. I settled into a rocking chair, ready to connect with spirit, only to find that my head started to feel like it had been stuffed into a cardboard box padded with cotton wool. The house was rented to Lizzy and was one of a row of 1900 terraced houses. I gently explained in response to the puzzled look she was giving me, that there was a little bit of activity and suggested that I dealt with it before we started. The problem with working as a medium in such circumstances, is that you get very faint connections from the sitters 'loved ones' because the astral dwellers are magnetised to you. There is so much activity, that you have to resolve the haunting before you can access the link you anticipated. Lizzy laughed and said she wasn't surprised. At night, she heard men's' voices whispering in her ear and her young son would regularly rush into her bedroom, terrified by visions he was seeing. The thought did cross my mind, that some folk will but up with an extreme situation such as this, to the point where spirit will get a resolution, despite them. This was just what had happened in this case as I was about to be shown as the hour wore on.

I worked silently to cleanse the whole terrace of houses and, for the first time in this book, I use the word cleanse, as I was aware of such a cacophony of beings, that I worked to invite every discarnate energy, into the vortex of light, and desperately sort of 'threw the book' at them, in an understanding sort of way!! Somehow also, Lizzy still got her sitting, but her family's determination from beyond the veil had made this possible as it certainly wasn't my energy level.

How did I conclude that this was the major reason for my visit?

a) Spirit knew I would be in the vicinity on that day

b) Lizzy had already made her decision on her future in a very difficult situation, her loved ones fully knew this and simply took the opportunity to give her evidence of survival and provided evidence that the path she had chosen was to be steep and rocky.

A general consideration to bear in mind also, is that with the more recent trend to rent houses such as Lizzys, the history of activity within the house becomes unsure, as it has many more changes of tenancy over time. It becomes more difficult to assess how spirit activity may have influenced tenants and, surprisingly, how tenants might have influenced their neighbourly astral dwellers. Dwell on this yourself for a while…

Chapter 12

Attachments and exorcisms

Spirit Writer

WE WISH to speak on exorcisms. The very word exorcism seems to strike a note of terror in the hearts of you human beings. However, it hasn't been helped, historically, by mans' portrayal.

We mean to explain the fundamentals of the skill of exorcism, by demonstrating how the human aura can be transgressed by thoughts and thought forms, but not, in any negative or enduring way, by spirit.

You, in everyday life, can be influenced by the thoughts of others. They can pierce us with their focus, and often you mistake this ingress, for your own mood, so rule number one, if you are experiencing lowness of mood or negativism, chances are that it is someone elses' thoughts influencing you, so perhaps you will be good enough to visualise cleansing (exorcising?) your energy field and throwing the gold mantle of protection over yourself.

In your everyday living, you will be influenced by others energies in close proximity. Sensitives are prone to having their energy momentarily taken from them by a weaker source, but overall, you have power and might over your own spirit field. You can have influencing energies, yet these are most likely to be the positive guides and helpers, in a supportive role, entering your field as needed. Our writer will recount a rare attachment she experienced, but as she now knows, good came of it, otherwise we would never have allowed her the experience. When a healer / rescuer places their hands within your spirit field, they will magnetically disperse any uninvited thought forms. Its quick, it's calming and it's performed with love.

Taking up spirits point about how the living can affect us. I will commence this chapter by asking the reader to reflect on how others in life, can affect the tone of our mood either by the topic of conversation or by their attitudinal behaviour. A good example would be when someone has a negative opinion on something or someone; it will immediately bring the conversation to a low level unless it is instantly moved on to a lighter note. In the same way, others can affect us simply by being in close contact, leaving us feel negative or drained. It's not going to last long because it simply is not us, the real person. So we have a trespass into our energy field and we deal with it in our own way. Generally, we make decisions based on the experience and probably avoid such negative approaches in the future.

When we are practising mediums, psychics, healers and sensitives, we can be affected to a stronger extent. The best reason for this is that we are in the business of helping others, sometimes in their twilight world and I'm still talking of the living! Whereas a later chapter gives advice on disciplined living as a sensitive, this chapter serves to illustrate how the process of exorcism can be used to deal with a simple thought or a more resistant thought form.

I was recently contacted by another medium. I arranged to talk through the problem on my return from a late evening visit to a row of terraced houses. I felt an urgent need to contact her, despite the lateness of the hour I noticed by my watch, as I left the clients house. Although home wasn't too far away, I spoke urgently into my mobile, telling this friend in need than in ten minutes, I'd be near a landline and not to go to bed, but to phone me then. Quickly home, I made a hot mug of tea as I ditched my outdoor clothing and headed for the telephone.

Sally had met up with a 'friend' who ate at her expense and talked at her expense some two days ago. This friend as usual, spoke about her dark days and her troubles, as she ordered everything on the café menu, to be paid for out of Sally's dwindling resources. Sally had a cuppa and simple cake. It became apparent that this lady had influenced Sally's mood, as she was so low since the meeting and had heavy responsibilities to meet the next day. I suggested that the lowness wasn't hers and that I would send her absent healing straight away. I directed her to retire to her bed and called in a band of spirit helpers to assist. I found myself sending pure yellow and gold through to her and knew that she was benefiting. The next morning I contacted her for a very different reason! I had sensed as I prepared breakfast, a lowness of mood around me. I quickly realised that I had an attachment and so I went outside and dealt with it. It was momentarily unpleasant and it was tenacious. I then telephoned Sally despite the early hour and she eagerly described the wonderful healing and how great she felt for today's workload! I described the exorcism in the healing and she was given a clear message through her Mediumship, that I was absolutely right. She said that she had asked her soul for help at the time as she was so low and desperate. Her soul did a great job. Do actively love your soul, it can separately work to assist you on life's path.

Earthbound (astral) souls can affect us with their sympathetic attachment to similarly placed individuals upon this earth; alcoholics, sexual deviants, compulsives and particularly depressives. My heart goes out to those in a depressed state. All the baser addictions and deviant practices can be enhanced by souls in this sphere, still affected by their previous memories and conditions. This is why we should look at the aspect of attachment, in varying forms of control. I will not deal with complex mental health issues in this booklet, save to say that when I have the merest suspicion of Mental Health issues, I direct sufferers to their General Practitioner. Some will give a history of existing mental health problems on careful questioning, so bear in mind that in countries where General Medical Practitioners exist, then they should be updated by their patient on what they are doing health-wise.

I have had clients stating that others are sending horrible things to them. Often the problem is our belief that this can be done, but our helpers are equal to others malevolent practices. If a client feels cursed this way, they need to change their belief. I will, on occasion, give healing to this type of clients' energy field, on the basis that I am a healer and the client can choose to accept or refuse. I know that as I place my hands within their aura, it will be beneficially cleansed, particularly if reason returns to their thoughts!

In my experience, those most commonly presenting with 'attachments' often hearing voices that are persistent, are those with unresolved mental health issues. If voices are persistent and repetitive, then this is not spirit. Voices actively directing us, talking over us and admonishing us is not the work of our spirit friends, so my advice is to direct them to their GP/ Medical Practitioner and bow out!

I am commonly asked whether we can take spirits home with us in rescue work and generally speaking, the answer has to be no.

If there is a feeling that energies remain attracted to us post-rescue, we should perform a simple detachment exercise. In general life, we get 'thought attachments' from others of our world, as illustrated through Sally's experience. We can feel them and as most mediums and sensitives will agree, it is a simple task to cleanse our energy fields and strongly visualise protection around us. If I feel, following a rescue, that some poor soul 'retains an interest in being around me' and they do not respond to a further rescue, I know then for sure, that the energy is a little more complex and I strongly visualise a little bonfire on my body, where I feel them (usually head) and follow this with a cleansing and protection exercise. It's not a big issue, providing you are disciplined in your calling and this is how I dealt with Sally's entity.

My Big Lesson

I was due to visit Stansted Hall in Essex, for the weekend. I had dashed from a particularly difficult haunting. I had visited the house in Liverpool on three occasions and, happily, the family involved still had utmost faith in me. The phenomena involved chidrens' toys being played with, train sets moving round the track by themselves and the poor little toddler of the family being upended out of his buggy! The third and final visit brought me 'face to face' with the perpetrator, a sad and suspicious little disabled lad, who had never known motherly love and was spiting the toddler in the only way he knew how. I spent an age with this child literally, and he would only agree to move on if I would guarantee to be there for him, should he wake to find that the nightmarish past still existed. He was anxious to continue to stay in the beauty of heaven, with his loving and willing new helpers, and the feeling of joy that he was being exposed to. He was worried because the feeling of joy was so alien to him that it must indeed be a dream. He felt that his new state was tenuous and fragile to the point that I suggested that he could consider himself adopted by me, until such time that he matured to find that Heaven was indeed finding him worthy to stay! This situation continued for some weeks, him throwing out a thought to make sure that I was still there, me sending encouragement to him and finding that he was growing in spirit a little more with every glimpse. Now, during my time at Stansted, I arrived with a headache which persisted until I gave a very inappropriate talk on why more theory should be devoted to rescue work in Spiritualism. The result was that one of the executive committee approached me later that day, giving wholehearted encouragement to the suggestion within the talk. My headache went and with it its cause, ie the attachment! Was 'the boy David' the attachment that felt so strongly, that no-one should have to endure the prolongation of misery, on the astral, due to a misguided belief that they weren't good enough for heaven? He was certainly strong enough a character to do it. Should I have adopted such an altruistic approach to supporting him beyond the physical?

***

My fervent hope that is that whilst reading this book, it has either encouraged you to work in the field of rescue, assisted you in your present work, or has at least confirmed that generally, you are blessed to undertake such an essential role. It may simply have helped your belief, that there has to be more to life than the physical world.

Chapter 13

Anecdotes to Cherish

The Social Club Visitors

IT WAS around 2004 and I, with a few nurse colleagues, had been invited to the wedding of a friend and her Medical Consultant fiancé. We nurses decided to visit the local School of Dance where the happy couple were members, in order to put together a few dance steps for the celebrations to come at the wedding. The reasoning behind this was that most people in their circle of friends, were avid dancers, and we certainly weren't going to let the side down. The school of dance was on the fringe of a Cheshire suburb that had grown to have its own shopping centre. The premises themselves were on the first floor and consisted of a huge dancehall, complete with an impressive and solid drinks bar running the width of the far end of the room. A series of small tables with seating, bordered the dance floor. At the near end to the entrance, a smaller area of the original hall was sectioned off by two wooden doors and designated space for beginners and private teaching. The double doors to the entrance at the top of the stairs were the heavy solid wood of the 1930s' with reinforced glass panels at eye level, to reveal the delights beyond. The door paint showed the evidence of differing ages, with chipped edges revealing colours of cream, red and originally a plain dark green

As I state at every opportunity, spirit will get you to where you are needed, and if you are in the vicinity of a haunted building, then as a rescuer, the job is yours! As we were being shown around the premises, the young female employee explained that the first floor of the building, now this Dancing School, was at one time a Social Club hence its layout with the drinks bar. As she gave us the introductory tour, the club's owner came across and introduced himself, explaining that my talents had been spoken of, by our mutual friends the happy couple. It wasn't generally known, he stated quietly and staff weren't about to broadcast it, he continued, but all the younger female staff had experienced phenomena. They'd had their bottoms pinched from time to time, felt they were being followed, heard doors banging shut when the place had emptied and witnessed lights being switched on and off. Further information was given, as we completed our tour, and I had the situation pretty well summed up. Before our waltz lesson began, I took the opportunity to do a little work.

I 'saw' a group of three old drinking buddies, resplendent with pints of beer, sat at a circular table at the far end of the room, to the left of the bar as I faced it. I had a word with them, saying that their pranks were unsettling and unwelcome and that that their visits were too interactive and becoming altogether too lengthy.

At my next weekly class visit (Tango & Quickstep) the girls reported that the activity was still troublesome. I waited until the club closed for the night and directed my attention to the 'visitors.' I explained to them that I understood their enjoyment in meeting in old surroundings, and that last weeks chat to them had obviously been ignored. I said that I wasn't barring them from the premises but would if they didn't limit their interest. I explained that they should spend more time with family and friends on the other side, because they were avoiding the fact that they were physically dead. I exacted promises from all three, that there would be no further dabbling in this way in the physical world.

I left the club, crossing the road under the street lighting to where my car was parked. I was musing on what had just happened; sometimes even I wonder whether my imagination is too good. I decided that the feedback on my next visit would be the acid test and soon got on with my working week. Dance night soon came around one week later and deliberately first through the doors (Waltz and Foxtrot tonight) the barmaid rushed up to me, took my arm silently and walked me across the dance floor and in behind the bar. There, just as she had found it on the floor, below the till, was a freshly drunk pint pot, with the frothy remains of Boddingtons Beer, sliding down from the rim! "Well!" she said, incredulous at the sight, "The cheeky b……'s couldn't even wash up after themselves."

The one that got away

I rarely give up on a rescue mission, but I have the grace to recount an attempt some years back, when I was given a mission that I never really accomplished. The place was right, the stuck soul was correctly identified, but I reckoned without his guile. Today I may have handled it differently, possibly with more experience to hand. As however, it's one of only two that I can recount as failures so far, perhaps that is a realistic success rate. I only know that I travelled up and down the M62, testing such hypotheses as shutting down at a certain point, hoping we'd be 'off his radar,' I gave up on expecting fuel expenses after the second visit. I took students with me and was probably just fuelling this souls need to be noticed and a need to be in control. I sometimes think I'd like to make a return visit, but I imagine that family finally had enough of me as well! I wonder what they're experiencing these days.

The one that got away, for now......

I decided to end this chapter with something that happened very recently. In fact it's an unexpected last minute addition. So firstly I wish to share a scenario that has, as yet to be concluded. I had been in Liverpool, seeing clients and on my way home to Cheshire, intended to call in on a lady with a spirit visitor. She currently lives in rented rooms, awaiting her house being refurbished. When I spoke with her the previous week, she described a teenager in spirit who had 'adopted' her as a mother figure. He was coming too close, literally, and as she is blessed with strong psychic senses, felt it was becoming uncomfortable. She cited an incident recently where she had argued with her partner, and the young lad had managed to scratch him, in retaliation! I explained to Rita that the situation needed addressing sooner rather than later. Her partner had been sceptical prior to this incident and was now experiencing sensations of dampness falling on him, during his time in bed at night. Now, goodness only knows just what antics this youngster has been attempting in his immaturity, I leave it to you to conjecture! As I neared the address, I saw clairvoyantly, this youngster, trying to challenge me. He stubbed out a cigarette and virtually said "Bring it on, come on just you try it." I knew then that he was attempting to block my visit. I found the building and on knocking, Rita came to the door and apologised but she had emailed me to change dates. Now, call me cynical, but I could have said that since I was there at the door, then in only a short time we could resolve this, yet I knew that this wouldn't be acceptable. I knew that the influence by the young man had worked. I will now await the next approach, when things are happening that no-one would put up with, even a surrogate mother...

Chapter 14

Staying positive

YOUR SPIRIT/SOUL body is a fine matrix of lines of energy, moulding the very cell structure of your body and storing every happening, good and not so good.

This Spirit/Soul body responds to stimuli. Its fine lines are connected with the autonomic nervous system. It responds to positive and negative stimuli and will react rapidly to light / colour vibrations which can mend, heal, balance, uplift and motivate the mind. This is the Human Energy Field (Aura) that can assimilate positive or negative thought energies from another human and later, I will be discussing the importance of removing trespassing negative energy, as distinctly different from dealing with your home grown thoughts! The mind is a fickle, non-tangible part of us which can alter our version of reality, simply by us listening to another human and adopting their way of thinking or their words of persuasion. We spend a major part of our lives, mastering the three planes of existence, peculiar to this Earthly Life. When we have suitably mastered them, we move on to the contribution phase, when we give back of our wisdom and expertise, just as I am in this book.

One of the planes of existence is the Mental Plane. The other two are the Physical and the Emotional Planes. We master the Physical Plane in connection with what we eat, where we live and how we generate income, to the eventual point where material things start to mean less to us, as we self-actualise.

We master the Emotional Plane when we appreciate that each and every one of us has differing ways of growing and seeing what is important to our world. It is never truer than when we share our life with another, then the balance of power should become equal in an ideal world, but an ideal world is not in existence. When we have the opportunity to move on with our lives, whether from personal relationships, or work relationships, to new experiences or new vocations, then we should ideally leave the past with honour, rather than forced circumstances, but human nature being what it is, it's not often achievable.

The Mental Plane however, is the condition which we have to master on a daily basis! Our minds are full of work and home commitments, hopes and dreams.

We carry guilt, uncertainty, arguments, lost friendships, unhappiness and frustrations, all bordering on the Emotional Plane, but made up of our thoughts and emotional responses. What is worse is that if we're not careful, we carry the more negative aspects of yesterday, into the new day as it begins. So towards the end of this chapter, I will suggest to you that you lie to your mind each morning and experience instant happiness!

We do need to work through any problems, everyone has to. We can experience sadness one day and too easily it will be the first thought popping into our head the next morning. It's just as though we have to go through a mental checklist of what continues to worry us. At some point in our reasoning, we have to put some situations under the heading of 'work in progress' and decide what we can and can't change in our circumstances. Life actually has a way of resolving problems outside of your control but this takes some time, and rather than feel that we are responsible, inch by inch, for every change needed, it may be simpler to look at the up side of our position in life. Once you start feeling grateful for your life, then blessings will appear like magic, because you are starting to flow with your life's changing purpose. I always say that when your soul is in a boring or complacent place, it will concoct a new situation to experience. If you manage to flow with these changes rather than fear the unknown, perhaps demonstrate a childlike trust and see life as a seriously absorbing game, then your journey should take off more smoothly.

Others can make us feel inadequate, or vulnerable, but we are perfectly okay, as long as we 'like how we think' and don't try to live in another's life situation that might take our energy and thoughts. I have learned over the years that my best friend is my self (my soul). Good friends support us and make us smile; my 'self' does that.

No-one is ever 'centre stage' in a scenario. Why is it that others involved in our lives can be less successful in making us smile? Please remember that however others might act in their own interests, the outcome can still be favourable for us if, that is, we have the ability to respond to a situation by reflecting and recognising what is being given to us, by another's actions. Sometimes another's actions have to happen, to allow changes in our lives. Sometimes a situation can occur simply to help us see what or who we don't want in our lives. The gain will come later, once Spirit (and our soul) has moved us to a place of comparative safety then balance will occur. Perhaps we should welcome and invite in, new beginnings, and see that that what we think is fear, loss and low self-esteem, is actually just a prelude to adjustment?

I was burgled last year. When I reflected that the only things taken were my two laptop computers, one very new, one very old, I realised that I had gotten off lightly and that my personal papers, bank cards and bits of jewellery hadn't been touched. What is more, my memory disk from my computer had been detached and left behind. The insurance company reimbursed me with two new laptops, virtually identical, and I saw straight away that another persons need to steal from me had all been tailored by Spirit, so that I might write this book between office and home, now having compatible software. The burglar was caught and is now receiving support with his drug habit…

With a view to maintaining a strong and positive daily attitude towards a constantly changing and challenging earthly life, we need to greet the day with a positive and uplifting approach. This is just like pouring a warm, golden glow into our auras and we are definitely entitled to feel this way. It is medicinal and nurturing. We are not about to live a lie, or be in denial!

It is deserved and it is preferred by your soul, because the soul only recognises positive energies. Think negative and you dim your light, you reduce your boundaries of possibilities and you lessen your connectivity with spirit. We are brave little energetic beings on this planet, working creatively with changes and experiences. Positive energy, positive thoughts and positive responses are strengthening, empowering and allow us to push our boundaries of trust and optimism. When we are feeling positive, we can ignite the spark in others, hence the saying 'laugh and the world laughs with you'.

Positive energy is also a pre-requisite for soul rescue and other psychic sciences; positive mood, confidence and uplifting thoughts will empower you to work strongly and effectively with the world of spirit.

Others thoughts can trespass in your aura

Negative energies or negative thoughts are self limiting and do not light up our lives. As with positive energy, negative energy is also transferable, and for this reason, we need to ensure that any negative thought is ours and not someone elses' in trespass, in your aura.

In the vibrational world of spirit, communication is by thought. We humans can of course also do this and thoughts can reach us from other humans. These thoughts can have a direct consequence on our mood as I explained in the chapter on exorcism. They can, as mentioned earlier, affect us to the point where they can alter our mood. The person doesn't need to be in our vicinity. Often, when I'm due to see a client for a private sitting, I will sense their mood of anxiety or grief. I send them a big pink love heart through the ether, and the feeling subsides. However much I usually know when something is affecting me, it can take us unaware.

So, when feeling low, the first action to take is to cleanse your energy field (self) *fig.1* by strongly visualising white light,

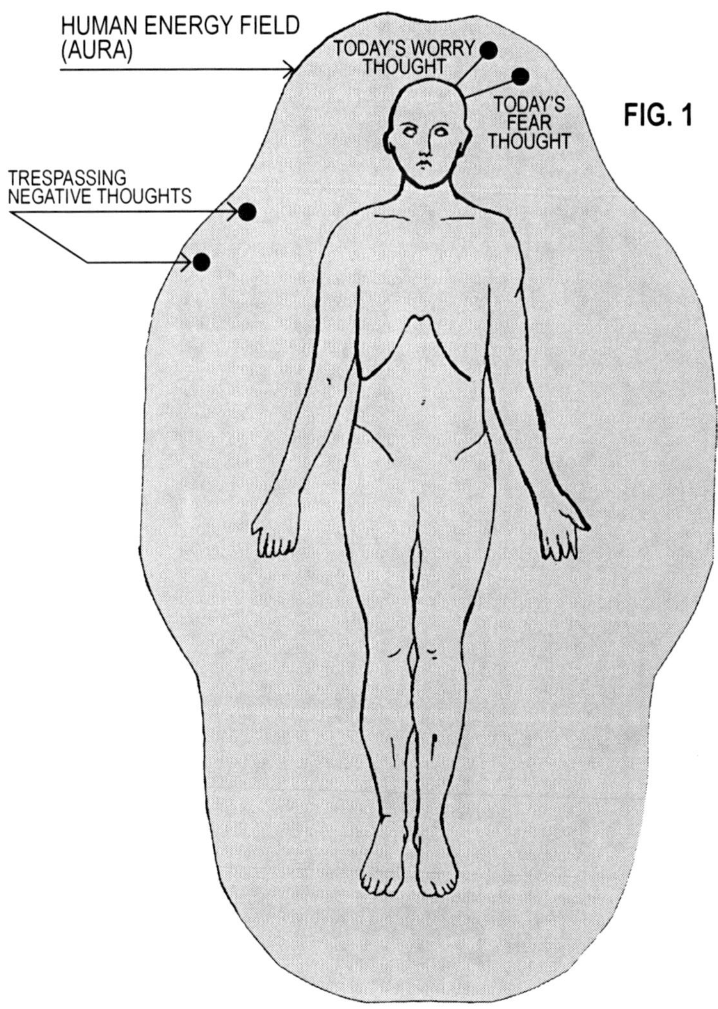

FIG. 1

coming in through the crown of your head and strongly 'see' it as a water level which is slowly leaving the body through the plug hole of your feet *fig 2* I'm saying this straight away, because it will rid you of an assortment of thoughts of the day, yours and others, quickly and efficiently.

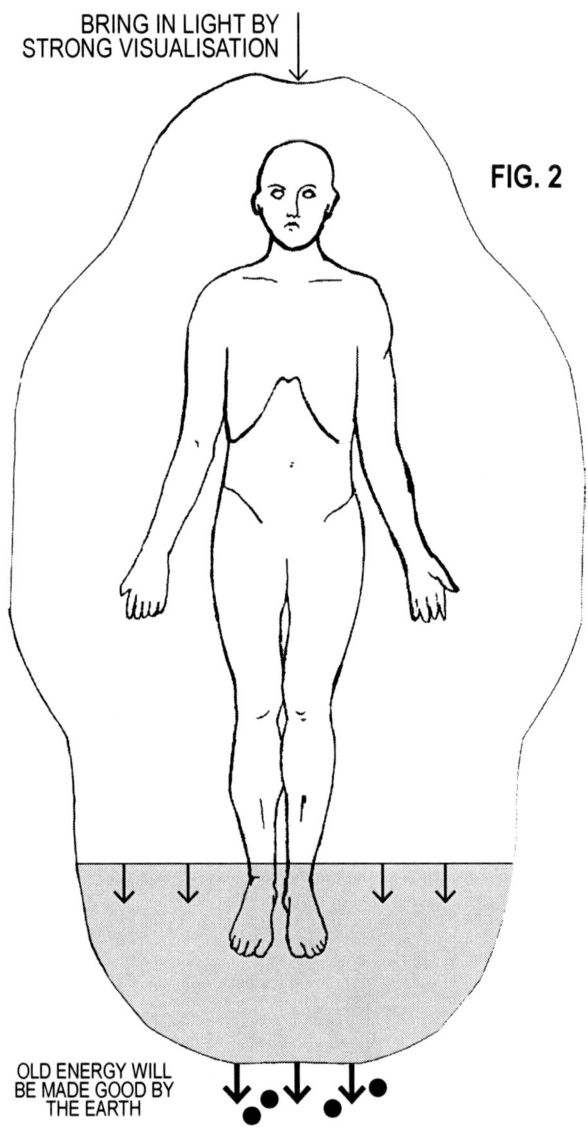

You can then visualise liquid brilliance (clear light) or a white light or colour, to pervade your aura and physical body. *Fig 3* You can draw this in through the crown of your head, breathe it into your aura or, as I sometimes do I visualise throwing a bucket of yellow paint at myself.

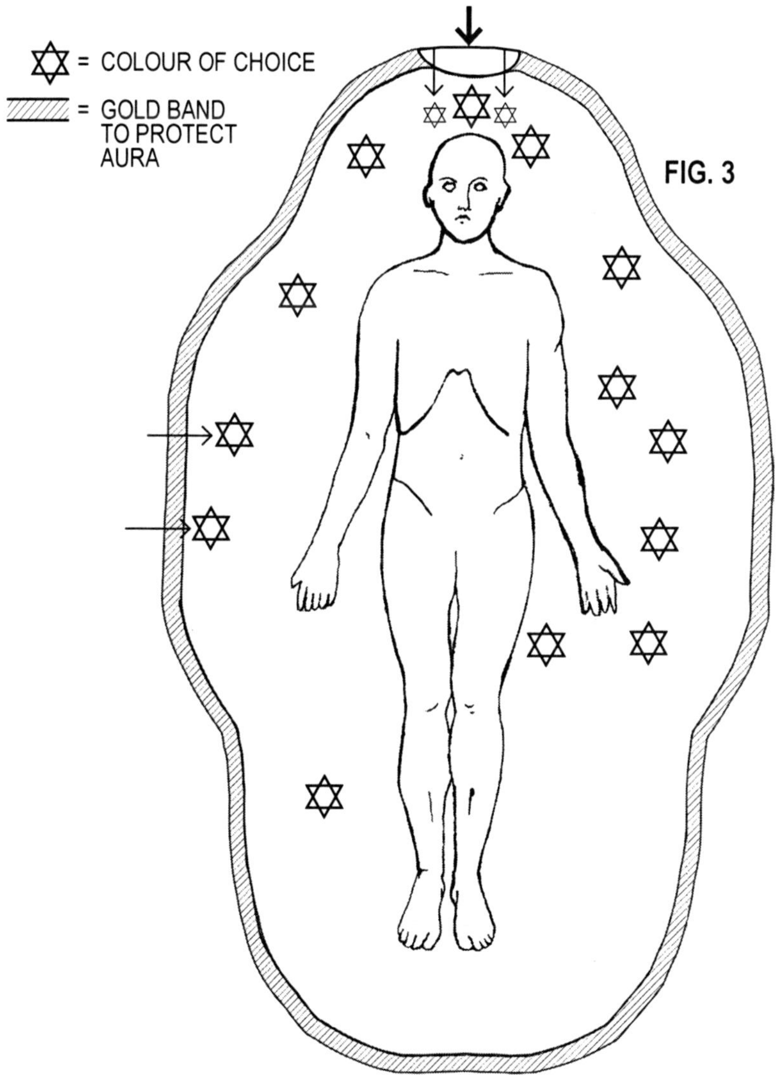

Colour is an instant mood changer

Colour is an energy frequency, and, the warm colours of the artists' palette are perfect for replacing this low energy, so then consider visualising filling the empty space in your body with the colour your mood requires. Try yellow, it is so uplifting (and wise) to visualise, or perhaps orange (red +yellow) as it brings the red strength to yellow wisdom to make you feel confident in tackling the day or the task ahead. Yellow is also very beneficial in promoting mental strength, as a medium, I find it a major colour in my daily repertoire.

Why have I launched straight into colour? Colour (vibrational energy) links the conscious with the unconscious and can change your feelings, simply by you wearing it, visualising it, breathing it in, or looking at it, it is instant!

If I have a pain, I will drink water, visualising it healing blue, going to the affected area and will feel the instant effect. Blue is the vibration of healing. Blue is good to reduce blood pressure, red will enhance the flow of blood and raises blood pressure.

Neutral position is rarely achieved but in its finest hour is a form of detachment, patience and peace, brought about by pure trust and love of life. The neutral colour of the palette is green. If I need to relax, I will visualise green or, go for a walk in the countryside. If you are feeling stressed, visualise the back of your body bathed in green. Green is also for growth, in all its forms.

So, leaving colour alone, let us look at the mind again. It is too easy to wake up in low mood, as we tend to bring to mind, our problems and responsibilities of the day, as well as yesterdays. Our mind accepts what we think, so there you are, a done deal! If we have to wait for our birthday or other celebration in order to be happy, then the tendency is to treat ourselves deliberately in the meantime, to help to raise our mood. I strongly argue against this, as it is expensive, bad for our health and is by no means permanent. However, become positive naturally and you will want less treats, so when you encourage yourself to be positive, it's great to enjoy and does not have to be followed by a low mood swing.

If you have experienced Positivity, and made it habitual practice to be so, then any change to a negative mood will be picked up quickly by you good 'self' and you will be encouraged to act swiftly to simply reverse it.

If you have ongoing problems with depression, please consult with your doctor on what your intention might be, in using natural methods for healing.

So, we are looking for consistent moods, for a better quality of life. Consistency means becoming balanced, neutral, Green!

If you fear the day and fear life, you loose so much quality time. If you place yourself in positive mode, then you instantly deserve it!

When you wake up, lie to your mind! Sing a happy song. I applaud the day; I clap my hands and thank those unseen helpers, for my blessings to come. I trust in them, as they are the guardians of our earthly journey. This is not your home; it's a place of experiencing just how creative you can be. If you want to fly through this life, simply stand still and silently call your helpers to you. Ask for help to keep you positive. Wear vibrant warm colours and visualise yellows and orange.

We are here to experience happiness. Positivity also comes from non-reacting in difficult circumstances. If we, by examining why something happened, rationalise the situation and see the higher picture, we also form the realisation of the lesson, the help that is in fact being given, the warning to go no further on a project for example. A friend was telling me, with more than a little exasperation, that every answer paper that she sent to her examiner, was sent back full of critical comments and the suggestion that she start again. Conversely, another course examiner was giving her top marks in a different topic. I was guided to tell her to stop wasting her time at present in the first course; Spirit wanted her to concentrate in the area where she was shown she was accepted. You are cosseted by your helpers, supported, directed, warned and essentially guided! Accept, listen, become one with the power behind your journey. When we are feeling low, we disengage from the higher energies, simple as that. We can still ask, pray, hope and remain beloved, but we fail to see the higher picture because the higher picture is too positive to behold.

When performing soul rescue, the astrally stuck, need to see your light shining bright and clear into their dull world, need to see a lovely gold auric light, just like a seasoned lifeboat crew member, throwing out a strong rescue rope, they are looking to you to give that positive glowing lifeline that they can trust. To glow, you need positivity Please, finally, remember that when you are around others who are negative, you need to examine just why you are there, and the effect they have on you. If you have to be consistently in their company, you will have to protect yourself constantly but more of that in the next chapter.

So, to recap, lie to your mind, trust and actively cleanse your energy field. Use colour and actively notice it in your waking happy positive life. If someone wishes to make you feel negative, and you can't change things then pity them and pray that their helpers might bring the changes they need.

Chapter 15

Living sensitively

THERE IS an ever increasing interest in matters psychic. Television programs provide a broad range of psychic information. The lovely ability to provide Magnetic Healing has spread via Reiki systems, making practitioners more sensitive. As they transfer energy to the needy, it the increases the vibratory rate in the healers' Human Energy Field (HEF) through the ability to increase the magnetic energy available.

Most, if not all Complimentary and Alternative Medicine (CAM) workers, will be Sensitives because of the work they do. We then have the groups being actively taught to use their psychic powers, or will increase the flow of Kundalini via yoga, meditation and the like. We have the more formal platform for using natural gifts in Spiritualist Churches and organisations, teaching well and giving credence, underpinned knowledge and written qualifications to Mediums and Healers. It's not a closed door; anyone with the right intention can enter.

Living as a Sensitive requires careful handling. Many years ago I was reminded that discipline was everything to success and this remains the watchword, increasingly more so. A working sensitive not only requires a robust and confident approach to their work, but the discipline involved is in ensuring that we keep such a positive working field and, more importantly, that we know when to rest it! When we are working with our spirit bodies, it is a delicate state to place ourselves in and not compatible, for prolonged periods of time, with good physical health. When we talk about discipline, it involves a healthy respect for the law of energy transference.

In the previous chapter, we touched on an exercise to cleanse and re-energise the aura (Human Energy Field) what follows, are situations where your energy is at risk of being lowered, and, although it will regenerate within hours if you generally are disciplined, a regularly depleted energy field will impact on your health. In my work as a platform medium, I arrange my commitments around my energy fields' ability to replenish itself. I know that working in a Spiritualist Church service requires me to be quiet during the hours preceding it, and so I'll potter around, doing minor things and tying up loose ends. When I give private sittings, I'll limit the amount I book, in accordance with my comfort zone. I'll protect myself by visualisation in most situations where I interact with the general public, because I know that my tendency is to embrace life and that attitude itself is enough to attract those whose' auras are weak. If I'm aware that I have a haunting to resolve, I'll attempt to make it the last task of the day as I mentioned in an earlier chapter, because through experience of past years, chances are you are going to use your auric energy to a greater degree.

Discipline outside of the home

When entering a crowded place, where anyone passing by can take your energy (strong flow to weak flow is a natural law) prepare by visualising a barrier around your energy field, gold, band, brick wall or black cloak are examples *(fig.3)*.

Consider also, visualising your energy field cling-wrapped tightly around you, to calm and protect the major energy centres and conserve your auric energy *(fig.5)*

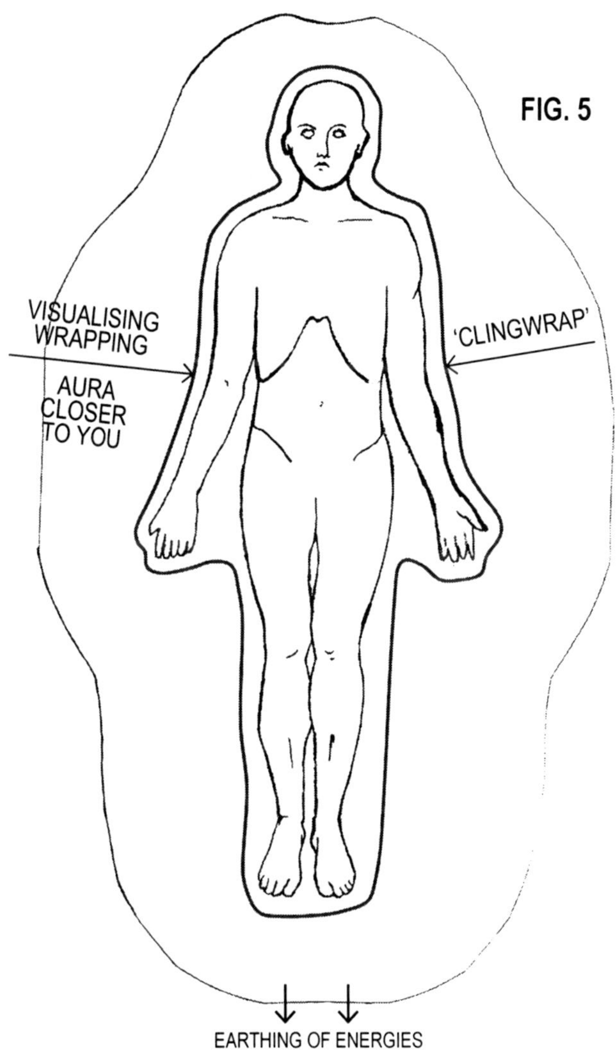

I well remember meeting up with an acquaintance in a shopping centre. I was aware that she was developing psychically, and true to her nature, not only did she quiz me as to my life, but I could feel that she was sending psychic fronds, trying to trespass into my aura to gain information from and about me. I visualised my aura shrinking to wrap tightly around me and the acquaintance lost interest in our conversation!

When in contact with the needy, the grieving and the unwell, then do the same, as they again, will have an unconscious need to find energy that someone else is generating. We, through our generation of energy, naturally, pre-digest this energy to work in subtle ways for our body's health. Reiki healers, for example, will channel this energy to those needing a boost to specific areas of the body. They will work to bring in extra energy rays, digest or convert them and flow them into the client. The clients body will recognise this energy and intelligently distribute it as needed.

Discipline in rescue work. Prior to working in rescue, bring the magnetic energies of the earth, by visualisation, up, through the soles of your feet and into your energy Field (*fig.4*).

Post working, cleanse your field, renew and strengthen (*fig.2*)

The Value of Self-Discipline When In Close Company

I have loving and patient helpers who have over the years, saved me from myself by giving me situations where my energy has momentarily been drained. By so doing, they have alerted me to potential future problems so that I might plan the best ways to practice living sensitively. Recently I met a friend for lunch. She brought her mum along and as I sat at the table, I felt myself very suddenly drained of energy. I was so weak that I couldn't find the energy to move away. My friend noticed this and I signalled not to worry. This violent loss to my aura resolved within 10 minutes of saying goodbye. Mum looked heaps better when she left.... A Sensitive must learn to be constantly mindful of protecting the Aura. This is not a notion and you must fully participate in visualising the form of protection this takes. Ideally, the ritual of cleansing and recharging the energy field should be repeated as needed during the day. (see figs. 2,3.) What you do often you do well, which will make it a pleasure rather than a pain!

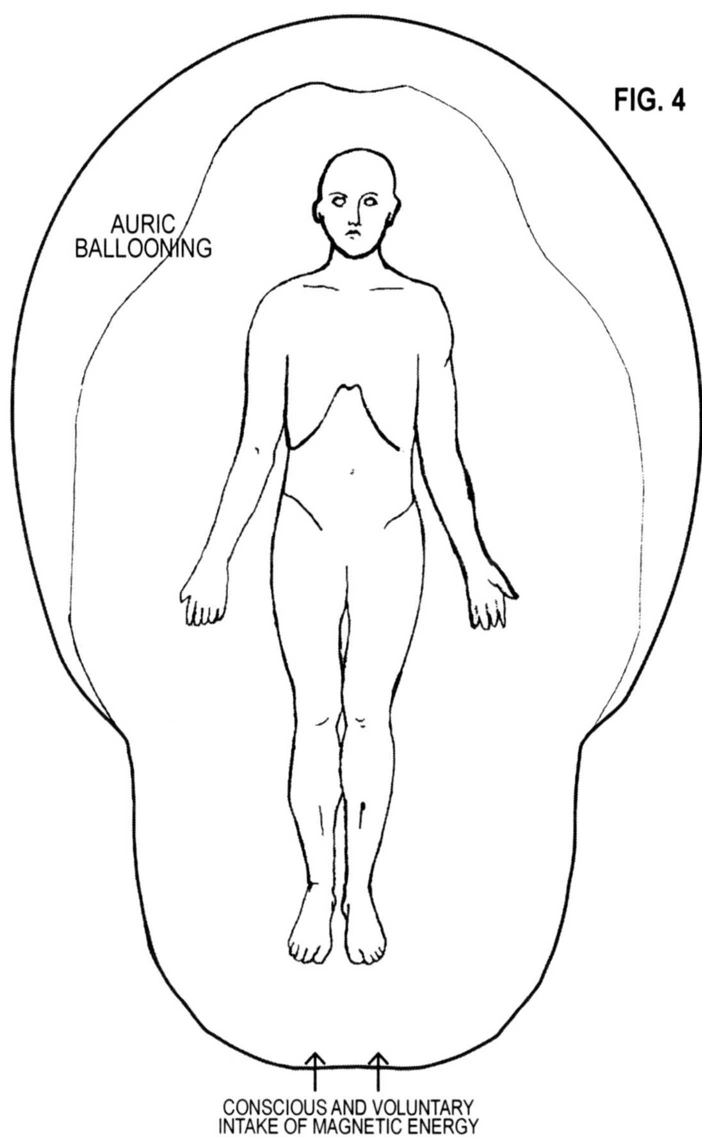

Sensitives need to remain optimistic and optimally 'charged up.' So why do it and how? We can do this intentionally as described in *fig 3* and we can do it by positive and happy thought, as described in the previous chapter. We can enhance this with laughter, singing and loving feelings.

I mentioned in the introduction, that we are all energy, both positive & negative. Earth conditions aren't kind to the HEF when it is given exposure. We share this earth Plane with everyone else and, as it is a plane of mental, emotional and physical being, then we can be affected by others thoughts, emotions and need for physical strength.

Therefore we not only need (eventually) to be true to our own version of real thought, and strong enough emotionally, to know what we will accept in a partner or friend, but in the shorter term (and immediately when the need arises,) we must check out whose thoughts and emotions we are harbouring, by energy field cleansing *fig 2*

Many Sensitives will feel low inexplicably at some point of the day. Restful meditation need not take long and will recharge us beautifully. If it persists, then cleanse and recharge and repeat if necessary.

If you are ever saddened by someone's' behaviour towards you, perhaps by grief or by a weepy situation, then cry for a short while, tell yourself you are entitled. However, having done this healthy thing, sit quietly for five minutes because this has momentarily acted on your aura as a shattered windscreen would and you need putting back together. Speaking of windscreens, if you have had a difficult driving experience or tiresome journey, you will need to re-compose yourself. When you eventually retire to sleep, 'shut down' as in *fig.5.* If you experience difficulty in moving into deep sleep, such as I do after late evening working, place a red scarf or garment over your feet and place Red Jasper crystals near the lower part of your body.

Over time, you will recognise the lessons being learned, whether they are the need to cleanse, protect, reduce alcohol or caffeine drinks, meditate when the feeling comes upon you or avoid argumentative personality types. Loud music, or anything that arouses extremes of feelings or penetrates your aura in discomfort, you will become aware of. Know how you best function, as a sensitive whilst still in human mould!

Chapter 16

Template: Letter to Estate Agents & Housing Associations

LET THE Buyer be Scared? The Implications, Rights and Responsibilities in Managing the Problem of Haunted & Stigmatised Buildings, during the Transfer of Occupation by Sale or by Let.

This area of real estate is a growing issue for three prominent reasons. The first and most obvious one is the increasing investment in property prices globally and the need to maximise investment potential.

The second reason supports the first, in that in The USA, the problem of Haunted and Stigmatised Buildings (H&SB) has produced a decided case *Stambovsky v Ackley* which highlighted the need to fully disclose information and that the onus was not on the buyer to find the full facts.

In *Reed v King the* Stigmatism of murder committed in the house, resulted in the buyer eventually, on appeal, rescinding the contract and seeking damages. Both Seller and Agent were aware of the murders and knew that *"event materially affected the market value of the house when they listed it for sale"* The loss was cited as 15% of the market value to the purchaser!

In New South Wales, in the Gonzales Case, L.J.Hooker sold a property in Sydney that was the subject of a triple murder, and did not disclose the fact. The dispute with the purchasers was settled and action was taken against the Agents. In The USA it is Law in 31 states, that such information must be disclosed.

The third reason is, that we are becoming much more aware and interested in psychic matters, as a nation and, psychic manifestations are on the increase. In turn, this is has led to an increase in the number of psychics & dabblers around. Importantly the increase in manifestations is related to the increased number of tragic addictive deaths where support has been lacking.

Deaths by violence & murder compound the problem, where the disturbing history leaves the property stigmatised.

(Let them know how the problem affects occupiers &, what the legal experts conclude)

The Effects

The effects of haunted and stigmatised buildings on individual buyers and tenants, depends on the strongly varying perceptions of individuals. Prejudice, fear, superstition, irrationality and religious beliefs will all impact on the desirability of a property.

Whether to disclose or not? Most authors conclude that it is good practice to "disclose what is known". As one American expert stated, *"if a buyer is to be relied on to ensure they are not buying a haunted or stigmatised building, who ya gonna call?"…..*

(Let them know your previous experience with how bad it can get)

The Benefits of 'Cleansing'

The effect of earth-bound souls on families can range from frank annoyance to ill health, from an inability to settle in a property to an inability to stay in it! I am called upon to resolve a wide variety of manifestations. One of the more frequent is where souls are making their presence felt in order to get help and this can rise to poltergeist level, with objects being thrown, audible footsteps, banging doors & shaking beds!

My regular 'haunts' so to speak, cover North Wales, Greater Manchester, Cheshire & Merseyside. I have tackled a 'whole street' haunting, in Macclesfield taking with me a group of students to assist! In that case, the father in the house, mainly affected, had suffered for years with a sore throat, culminating in his having a tonsillectomy. Despite this, his sore throats persisted. I identified a soul with a severe throat problem and on removal; the fathers' sore throats also went.

Three years ago I visited a house in North Manchester, where Souls actively stopped the resident from using the front room! When children are terrified by spirit, I make it a priority to visit, recognising the importance of stability in the home, luckily children soon adapt to more normal surroundings. However, it is astounding how many hauntings will be accompanied by spirit children, who come to play amid the existing turmoil, as though they are attracted by the situation.

Last year I cleansed a shop with living premises in Frodsham. The owner couldn't live in the place and was constantly tearful but, following my visit, she truly bonded with the property and is now completely happy.

I have tackled divided houses, where souls moved from one area to another in vast buildings, which had been divided into flats etc., not an easy one!

New alterations and refinements in older properties and, surprisingly, new housing builds on farmland, will bring problems from 'ex inhabitants'. I have found whole terraces of houses in Liverpool have been prone to problems, linked by attic thoroughfares. The longer those problems are left or ignored, the greater the potential for other earth bound souls to become attracted to the area.

I visited a bungalow in Weston Village recently and, apart from a more recent problem, I encountered an 18th Century horseman who was a strong residual energy and a true gentleman. I requested that he drove around this bungalow in future and not through it & he did just that, so, no more problems there!

Some manifestations are simply the result of loved ones wanting to get a message of love and support to the occupier. Faced with this situation, I pass on the message faithfully and everyone feels better!

Conversely, I recently had a call from a Council tenant in North Wales and on being given the history, sensed an earth bound soul of a teenager, I sensed that death occurred by hanging, found to be correct on questioning the tenants further. Rather more uniquely, I found a room full of distressed animal souls - a previous tenant had been convicted for animal cruelty & had kept an assortment of animals in the room I had worked in.

Finally, where there is a stigma due to murder or violence, I would advise that there is a real need to visit, cleanse and ask for a blessing from above.

(Tell them your experience in keeping work confidential)

Confidentiality

In my work, it is vital that all work is kept low key and absolutely confidential. The risk is one of the houses becoming stigmatized if the neighbours find out. I have, for most of my working life, been a Senior Nurse; the last 6 years of my career were spent as a Night Services Manager. I managed all services, deputized during night hours, for the CEO of South Manchester Hospitals Trust, and refined my skills and capabilities in all areas of dealing with the general public. I know how to deal with awkward situations and I know to help the distressed. I operate on the basis that everything is confidential unless it is explicit to publish.

When a house visit is made, it is kept low key, professional and pleasant. Within Spiritualism, there are relatively few mediums with the specialist skills and experience in Soul Rescue. Some sensitives can feel it is too 'dark' an energy for them to work in.

(Don't forget to add in your own unique expert skills)

Expert Skills

During my training as a medium, I have been assessed for my ability to work in Churches giving accurate and sensitively delivered information to a hall of complete strangers, many of whom are grieving or sorrowful. With impending legislation for Mediums, the Accreditation Scheme with the Spiritualists National Union is a two year course designed to give credence to established and new Mediums, to afford protection for us in our work for Spirit.

As I wrote earlier, there are relatively few of us doing this work in Spiritualism & so my experience stems from the need to provide such a service on a very regular basis. I am of the strong belief that all souls deserve to be released to follow their eternal journey and that the service that I perform is vital for the quality of their spirit existence.

Penny can be contacted by email for details of courses and lectures available
penny.barber@ntlworld.com

Lightning Source UK Ltd.
Milton Keynes UK
UKOW030040101012

200325UK00002B/207/P